LangGraph Unlocked

A Complete Guide to Building Intelligent Agents
and Multi-Agent Systems for Next-Gen AI
Workflows

James Acklin

Copyright Page

Table of Contents

Preface 5

Chapter 1: Understanding Intelligent Agents 7

    1.1 What Are Intelligent Agents? 7

    1.2 Anatomy of an Agent... 11

    1.3 Types of Agents 16

Chapter 2: Introduction to Multi-Agent Systems 23

    2.1 Key Concepts of Multi-Agent Systems............................ 23

    2.2 Benefits and Challenges of Multi-Agent Systems 28

    2.3 Real-World Applications of Multi-Agent Systems............. 33

Chapter 3: Graph Structures in AI 38

    3.1 Basics of Graph Theory 38

    3.2 Modeling Relationships and Workflows with Graphs 43

Chapter 4: What is LangGraph? 54

    4.1 Overview of LangGraph Architecture 54

    4.2 Core Components 58

Chapter 5: Setting Up LangGraph 64

    5.1 Installation and Configuration 64

    5.2 Integrations with AI Libraries and Tools 69

    5.3 Introduction to LangGraph APIs.................................. 74

Chapter 6: Building Your First Agent in LangGraph......................... 81

    6.1 Step-by-Step Agent Creation 81

    6.2 Assigning Roles and Defining Goals 86

    6.3 Executing Basic Workflows 91

Chapter 7: Designing Multi-Agent Systems.................................. 98

    7.1 Creating Agent Networks and Hierarchies 98

    7.2 Inter-Agent Communication and Collaboration 104

    7.3 Task Allocation and Conflict Resolution 109

Chapter 8: Advanced Techniques in LangGraph............................ 116

8.1 Integrating Machine Learning and NLP 116

8.2 Reinforcement Learning for Adaptive Systems 121

8.3 Distributed Systems and Scalability 126

Chapter 9: Specialized Use Cases...133

9.1 Workflow Automation and Optimization.................................133

9.2 Multi-Agent Simulations for Research and Planning.............138

9.3 Industry-Specific Applications 144

Chapter 10: Performance Optimization and Debugging 150

10.1 Optimizing Graph Performance...150

10.2 Troubleshooting Multi-Agent Systems 155

10.3 Best Practices for Large-Scale Deployments....................... 160

Chapter 11: Trends in Intelligent Agents and Multi-Agent Systems .167

11.1 Emerging Technologies in AI Workflows...............................167

11.2 Future Prospects of Multi-Agent Systems 169

Conclusion 173

Preface

In the rapidly evolving world of artificial intelligence, intelligent agents and multi-agent systems have become cornerstones of innovation. These systems are not just theoretical constructs; they are transformative technologies that have redefined industries, from healthcare and finance to logistics and beyond. As AI workflows grow increasingly complex, the demand for robust frameworks to design, implement, and optimize intelligent agents has never been greater. It is in this context that **LangGraph Unlocked** emerges as a vital resource for practitioners, researchers, and enthusiasts alike.

The genesis of this book lies in a clear vision: to empower readers with the knowledge and tools needed to build sophisticated AI systems that are adaptable, efficient, and scalable. LangGraph, a graph-based framework for constructing intelligent agents and multi-agent systems, represents a significant step forward in this direction. By leveraging the inherent strengths of graph theory—interconnectivity, scalability, and dynamic adaptability—LangGraph enables users to create AI workflows that are both intuitive and powerful.

This book is structured to cater to a diverse audience. Whether you are a seasoned AI developer seeking advanced techniques or a newcomer eager to grasp the fundamentals of intelligent agents, *LangGraph Unlocked* offers a guided journey. The content progresses from foundational concepts to hands-on applications, interspersed with practical examples, industry insights, and real-world use cases. Each chapter builds upon the last, ensuring a cohesive learning experience.

Our goal is not just to teach you how to use LangGraph but to inspire you to think creatively about the possibilities of intelligent agents and multi-agent systems. We delve into the theory and practice of AI, explore the nuances of graph-based modeling, and provide actionable guidance for designing, deploying, and optimizing your systems. From simple agents that perform basic tasks to complex multi-agent ecosystems solving intricate problems, this book covers it all.

As the field of AI continues to advance, we hope this book serves as a touchstone for innovation. The principles and techniques you'll encounter here are not confined to LangGraph alone—they are broadly applicable to the wider landscape of AI development. Our intention is to equip you with the skills and mindset necessary to navigate this dynamic domain with confidence and creativity.

Finally, we owe a debt of gratitude to the vibrant AI community, whose groundbreaking work has laid the foundation for this book. We also thank the early adopters and contributors to LangGraph, whose feedback and insights have been invaluable in shaping its development. This book is a reflection of our collective ambition to push the boundaries of what is possible with AI.

We invite you to embark on this journey with us. May *LangGraph Unlocked* not only illuminate the path ahead but also inspire you to envision new horizons.

Chapter 1: Understanding Intelligent Agents

1.1 *What Are Intelligent Agents?*

An intelligent agent is a system capable of perceiving its environment and acting upon it in a way that achieves specific objectives. This definition might sound straightforward, but it encapsulates a vast range of systems, from the simple to the incredibly complex. Intelligent agents lie at the heart of many modern technologies, and their applications are as diverse as chatbots, autonomous vehicles, and even stock trading systems.

To break this down, an intelligent agent typically consists of three primary elements: a way to perceive its surroundings (using sensors or data inputs), a mechanism to process that information (logic, rules, or machine learning models), and a method to act upon the environment to achieve a goal (via physical or digital outputs).

Let's go through these ideas step by step, adding depth and examples to ensure a strong foundational understanding.

Perception

Perception is the first step for any intelligent agent. This involves collecting data from the environment through various sensors or inputs. For physical agents, such as robots or self-driving cars, sensors might include cameras, microphones, or LiDAR systems. For virtual agents, such as a chatbot, the "sensor" might be the text entered by a user.

Example: Virtual Assistant Perception

Consider a virtual assistant like Siri. When you speak, your voice is captured as an audio input (the sensor). The assistant then processes this data to understand what you said and what you might mean.

In programming terms, perception often involves receiving raw data and converting it into a format that can be analyzed. Below is a Python example demonstrating how a simple agent might process text input to recognize key commands:

```
# Example: Simple Perception in a Text-Based Agent
user_input = input("Enter your command: ").lower()

# Processing the input
if "weather" in user_input:
    print("Fetching the weather for you...")
elif "news" in user_input:
    print("Getting the latest news...")
else:
    print("I'm not sure how to help with that.")
```

This example shows a basic form of perception, where the agent "listens" to user input and categorizes it into actionable items. While basic, this is foundational to building more sophisticated agents.

Processing

Once an agent collects data, it must decide how to interpret it. This is where logic and algorithms come into play. Depending on the complexity of the agent, this might involve:

Rule-Based Systems: If-else logic where the agent responds to predefined scenarios. This is simple and fast but limited in adaptability.

Machine Learning Models: Algorithms that learn from data to make predictions or decisions. These models are far more flexible but require training and computational resources.

For instance, consider a stock trading bot. The agent must process real-time data from financial markets and decide whether to buy or sell. It may analyze historical trends, current prices, and external factors like news events.

Real-World Processing Example: Sentiment Analysis

A practical application of processing is analyzing the sentiment of a text input, such as classifying whether a tweet is positive, negative, or neutral. Here's how you might build a basic sentiment analysis tool using Python:

```
from textblob import TextBlob

def analyze_sentiment(text):
```

```
    analysis = TextBlob(text)
    sentiment = analysis.sentiment.polarity   #
Range: -1 (negative) to 1 (positive)

    if sentiment > 0:
        return "Positive Sentiment"
    elif sentiment < 0:
        return "Negative Sentiment"
    else:
        return "Neutral Sentiment"

# Example usage
user_input = input("Enter a sentence: ")
print(analyze_sentiment(user_input))
```

This example illustrates how agents can process text to extract meaningful insights. Such processing forms the foundation for more complex behaviors.

Action: Achieving Goals

After perceiving and processing, an intelligent agent takes action to influence its environment. This action could be as simple as displaying a message or as complex as controlling robotic arms in a manufacturing plant.

Actions can be immediate (like responding to a user query) or strategic (like planning a sequence of steps to achieve a goal). For example, an autonomous drone tasked with delivering a package must calculate the optimal route and adjust its actions based on weather conditions and obstacles.

Practical Example: Pathfinding in a Maze

Consider a robotic agent navigating a grid-based maze to reach a goal. Below is a simplified Python implementation of pathfinding using the A* algorithm:

```
import heapq

def astar(grid, start, goal):
    def heuristic(a, b):
```

```
        return abs(a[0] - b[0]) + abs(a[1] -
b[1])   # Manhattan distance

    open_set = []
    heapq.heappush(open_set, (0, start))
    came_from = {}
    g_score = {start: 0}
    f_score = {start: heuristic(start, goal)}

    while open_set:
        _, current = heapq.heappop(open_set)

        if current == goal:
            path = []
            while current in came_from:
                path.append(current)
                current = came_from[current]
            return path[::-1]

        neighbors = [(current[0] + dx, current[1] +
dy) for dx, dy in [(0, 1), (1, 0), (0, -1), (-1,
0)]]
        for neighbor in neighbors:
            if neighbor not in grid or
grid[neighbor] == 1:  # Skip walls
                continue

            tentative_g_score = g_score[current] +
1
            if tentative_g_score <
g_score.get(neighbor, float('inf')):
                came_from[neighbor] = current
                g_score[neighbor] =
tentative_g_score
                f_score[neighbor] =
tentative_g_score + heuristic(neighbor, goal)
                heapq.heappush(open_set,
(f_score[neighbor], neighbor))

    return None

# Example grid (0 = free space, 1 = wall)
```

```
grid = {(x, y): 0 for x in range(5) for y in
range(5)}
grid[(2, 2)] = 1  # Add a wall
start = (0, 0)
goal = (4, 4)

path = astar(grid, start, goal)
print("Path to goal:", path)
```

This example showcases how an agent can use algorithms to take actions that fulfill its goals.

An intelligent agent is more than a tool—it's a decision-maker designed to interact with its environment in purposeful ways. From the way it perceives the world, processes information, and takes actions, every element works together to achieve specific objectives. By combining these capabilities, agents can automate tasks, solve complex problems, and even operate in unpredictable scenarios.

1.2 Anatomy of an Agent

To understand what makes an intelligent agent work, it's important to break it down into its essential parts. An agent doesn't operate as a single unit; it functions as a system, with each part playing a specific role. If you're building an intelligent agent, you need to think about how it perceives, processes, and interacts with the world. This section provides a comprehensive look at the building blocks of an intelligent agent, how they fit together, and how to translate these concepts into code.

An agent consists of three fundamental components: **sensors**, **decision-making mechanisms**, and **actuators**. Surrounding these components is the **environment** in which the agent operates. Let's explore each part in depth to uncover how they interact and bring the agent to life.

The Environment: The World an Agent Operates In

The environment is the space where the agent exists and functions. It could be a physical environment, like a warehouse for a robot, or a digital environment, such as an e-commerce platform for a recommendation system. The environment provides the context for the agent's actions and is the source of all data it perceives.

For example, if we consider a self-driving car, its environment includes the road, traffic signals, pedestrians, and other vehicles. If we consider a virtual agent like a chatbot, its environment is the user interface and the data it interacts with (e.g., the user's queries).

In programming terms, the environment often defines the inputs that the agent must process and the rules or constraints it must follow.

Here's an example of how an environment could be modeled in a simple simulation:

class Environment:

```
    def __init__(self, grid_size):
        self.grid_size = grid_size
        self.state = [[0 for _ in range(grid_size)]
for _ in range(grid_size)]   # 0 represents an empty
space

    def update(self, position, value):
        """Update the environment with an agent's
position."""
        x, y = position
        self.state[x][y] = value

    def display(self):
        """Print the environment grid."""
        for row in self.state:
            print(" ".join(str(cell) for cell in
row))

# Example usage
env = Environment(5)
env.update((2, 2), 1)   # Place an agent at position
(2, 2)
env.display()
```

In this example, we've defined a grid environment where an agent can move. This structure allows us to simulate and test how an agent interacts with its world.

Sensors: How Agents Perceive Their Environment

Sensors are the agent's way of collecting information from its environment. They convert physical or digital data into inputs that the agent can process. These inputs can be as simple as binary data (e.g., a light sensor detecting on/off) or as complex as high-definition video from a camera.

For physical agents like robots, sensors include cameras, microphones, accelerometers, or LiDAR. For virtual agents, sensors are often data inputs, like user queries, API responses, or system logs.

Let's look at an example of a virtual sensor for a chatbot:

class Sensor:

```
    def __init__(self):
        pass

    def perceive(self, user_input):
        """Convert user input into a standardized
format."""
        return user_input.lower().strip()

# Example usage
sensor = Sensor()
input_data = "  What's the weather today?  "
processed_data = sensor.perceive(input_data)
print(f"Processed Input: {processed_data}")
```

This simple sensor standardizes user input, removing extra spaces and converting text to lowercase. In a more complex agent, sensors might preprocess data for natural language processing or image recognition.

Decision-Making

Once an agent has collected information through its sensors, it needs to decide what to do with that information. This is where decision-making comes in, often referred to as the agent's "brain." Decision-making can be implemented using rule-based systems, optimization algorithms, or machine learning models, depending on the complexity of the agent.

Let's consider a warehouse robot tasked with moving packages. Its decision-making process might involve evaluating the shortest path to its destination, avoiding obstacles, and prioritizing urgent deliveries.

Here's a simple rule-based decision-making example for a virtual agent:

class DecisionMaker:

```
    def __init__(self):
        self.rules = {
            "weather": "Checking the weather
forecast...",
            "news": "Fetching the latest news...",
            "time": "The current time is 2:00 PM.",
        }

    def decide(self, query):
        """Decide an action based on the query."""
        for key, response in self.rules.items():
            if key in query:
                return response
        return "I'm not sure how to help with
that."

# Example usage
brain = DecisionMaker()
query = "Tell me the weather."
response = brain.decide(query.lower())
print(response)
```

This example illustrates a simple rule-based system, where the agent selects a response based on predefined keywords. In more advanced systems, this decision-making process could involve probabilistic reasoning or deep learning.

Actuators: How Agents Act on Their Environment

Actuators are the agent's output mechanisms. They take the decisions made by the agent's brain and act on the environment to achieve a goal. For physical agents, actuators include motors, robotic arms, or speakers. For virtual agents, actuators might involve sending a message, generating a report, or triggering an API call.

Let's extend the earlier environment example to include an actuator that allows an agent to move within the grid:

class Actuator:

```
    def __init__(self, environment):
        self.environment = environment

    def move(self, current_position, new_position):
        """Move the agent within the
environment."""
        self.environment.update(current_position,
0)   # Clear old position
        self.environment.update(new_position, 1)   #
Mark new position
        return new_position

# Example usage
actuator = Actuator(env)
current_position = (2, 2)
new_position = (3, 3)
current_position = actuator.move(current_position,
new_position)
env.display()
```

In this example, the actuator moves the agent within the grid, updating the environment to reflect the agent's new position.

An agent is only as effective as the sum of its parts. Sensors gather data, decision-making mechanisms determine the next steps, and actuators execute those steps. By integrating these components, you can create agents capable of functioning autonomously in a variety of environments.

For example, if we combine the sensor, decision-maker, and actuator examples into a single agent, we get a simple system that can perceive user input, decide what to do, and act on that decision. Here's a combined implementation:

class Agent:

```
    def __init__(self, environment):
        self.sensor = Sensor()
```

```
        self.brain = DecisionMaker()
        self.actuator = Actuator(environment)
        self.position = (2, 2)   # Initial position

    def interact(self, user_input):
        """Complete agent interaction process."""
        processed_input =
self.sensor.perceive(user_input)
        decision =
self.brain.decide(processed_input)
        print(decision)

        # Example of moving the agent if a specific
command is given
        if "move" in processed_input:
            new_position = (self.position[0] + 1,
self.position[1] + 1)
            self.position =
self.actuator.move(self.position, new_position)

# Example usage
env = Environment(5)
agent = Agent(env)
agent.interact("move forward")
env.display()
```

This integrated example demonstrates how sensors, decision-making, and actuators work together to form the core functionality of an intelligent agent. From here, you can scale your agent to handle more complex inputs, decisions, and actions.

By understanding the anatomy of an agent, you now have the tools to build systems that not only respond to their environments but also actively interact with them in meaningful ways.

1.3 Types of Agents

When building intelligent agents, the approach depends heavily on the type of agent you're working with. Each type has its unique way of perceiving and interacting with its environment. These differences are determined by the complexity of their tasks, the level of autonomy required, and how they adapt to changing environments.

To help you understand how each type functions, we'll explore four major categories of intelligent agents: **Reactive Agents**, **Goal-Driven Agents**, **Utility-Based Agents**, and **Learning Agents**. For each, I'll provide an explanation, a real-world example, and a practical coding demonstration.

Reactive Agents

A reactive agent is the simplest form of intelligent agent. It operates purely on immediate perceptions and reacts to them based on pre-defined rules. Reactive agents do not store past experiences or anticipate future states; they only focus on what is happening now.

For example, consider a thermostat. Its sensor detects the current temperature, and based on pre-set rules, it either turns the heating or cooling system on or off. The thermostat doesn't remember previous temperatures or predict future changes; it just reacts to the current state.

Key Characteristics

Fast and lightweight because they don't need memory or complex computations.

Limited in flexibility since they cannot plan or adapt to new scenarios.

Code Example

Let's implement a simple reactive agent for controlling a light based on the presence of motion.

class ReactiveAgent:

```
    def __init__(self):
        self.light_on = False

    def sense_environment(self, motion_detected):
        """Perceive the environment to detect
motion."""
        return motion_detected

    def act(self, motion_detected):
        """React to the environment based on motion
detection."""
        if motion_detected:
```

```
            self.light_on = True
            print("Motion detected! Turning the
light ON.")
        else:
            self.light_on = False
            print("No motion. Turning the light
OFF.")

# Example usage
agent = ReactiveAgent()
agent.act(agent.sense_environment(True))   #
Simulate motion detected
agent.act(agent.sense_environment(False))   #
Simulate no motion
```

This simple program demonstrates how reactive agents work. They process immediate input and act accordingly without any additional context or memory.

Goal-Driven Agents

A goal-driven agent is more sophisticated. Instead of just reacting, it works toward a specific goal. It evaluates the current state of its environment and determines the best action to take to achieve its objective. This requires the agent to reason about its actions and make decisions based on how they will affect the outcome.

For example, a GPS navigation system is a goal-driven agent. The goal is to provide the shortest or fastest route to a destination. The system evaluates all possible paths and selects the best one based on current traffic conditions and distance.

Key Characteristics

Able to make decisions that prioritize long-term objectives.

Relies on a clear definition of the goal and a model of the environment.

Code Example

Let's build a goal-driven agent that navigates a grid to reach a target location.

class GoalDrivenAgent:

```python
    def __init__(self, start, goal, grid_size):
        self.position = start
        self.goal = goal
        self.grid_size = grid_size

    def move(self):
        """Move the agent one step closer to the
goal."""
        x, y = self.position
        gx, gy = self.goal

        if x < gx:
            x += 1
        elif x > gx:
            x -= 1

        if y < gy:
            y += 1
        elif y > gy:
            y -= 1

        self.position = (x, y)
        print(f"Agent moved to {self.position}")

    def has_reached_goal(self):
        """Check if the agent has reached its
goal."""
        return self.position == self.goal

# Example usage
agent = GoalDrivenAgent(start=(0, 0), goal=(3, 3),
grid_size=(5, 5))
while not agent.has_reached_goal():
    agent.move()
print("Goal reached!")
```

Here, the agent continuously moves one step closer to its goal. While simple, this is the foundation for more advanced systems, such as autonomous robots or delivery drones.

Utility-Based Agents

Utility-based agents go beyond achieving goals—they aim to optimize their outcomes. Instead of just reaching a destination, they evaluate various options and choose the one that provides the most benefit. This requires a **utility function**, which quantifies the desirability of different outcomes.

For example, an e-commerce recommendation system might suggest products based on a utility function that considers user preferences, item popularity, and potential profitability.

Key Characteristics

Able to evaluate trade-offs and make better decisions.

More complex due to the need for a well-defined utility function.

Code Example

Let's implement a utility-based agent that chooses the best path based on cost.

class UtilityBasedAgent:

```
    def __init__(self, paths):
        self.paths = paths   # Dictionary of paths
with costs

    def choose_best_path(self):
        """Select the path with the highest utility
(lowest cost)."""
        best_path = min(self.paths,
key=self.paths.get)   # Minimize cost
        print(f"Best path: {best_path} with cost
{self.paths[best_path]}")
        return best_path

# Example usage
paths = {
    "Path A": 10,
    "Path B": 5,
    "Path C": 8
}
agent = UtilityBasedAgent(paths)
agent.choose_best_path()
```

This agent evaluates multiple options and selects the one with the lowest cost, demonstrating the decision-making process of a utility-based agent.

Learning Agents

Learning agents represent the most advanced category. They are not limited to predefined rules or goals; they learn from their experiences and improve over time. This allows them to adapt to new environments and solve problems they've never encountered before.

For example, AlphaGo, the AI that defeated world champions in the game of Go, is a learning agent. It trained by playing millions of games and refining its strategies through reinforcement learning.

Key Characteristics

Adaptable and capable of handling dynamic environments.

Require significant computational resources and training data.

Code Example

Here's a simple learning agent that adjusts its actions based on feedback:

class LearningAgent:

```python
    def __init__(self):
        self.knowledge = {}

    def learn(self, situation, action):
        """Store the best action for a given
situation."""
        self.knowledge[situation] = action
        print(f"Learned: {situation} -> {action}")

    def decide(self, situation):
        """Decide the best action based on past
learning."""
        return self.knowledge.get(situation, "No
decision available")

# Example usage
agent = LearningAgent()
```

```
agent.learn("Low battery", "Recharge")
agent.learn("Obstacle ahead", "Turn right")

print(agent.decide("Low battery"))  # Output:
Recharge
print(agent.decide("Obstacle ahead"))  # Output:
Turn right
print(agent.decide("Unknown situation"))  # Output:
No decision available
```

This agent learns simple rules over time and uses them to make decisions. While basic, this structure is scalable to more complex learning algorithms.

Each type of agent—reactive, goal-driven, utility-based, and learning—has its strengths and limitations. Reactive agents are simple and fast, while learning agents are powerful and adaptive. By understanding these types, you can choose the right approach for your specific application, whether it's building a chatbot, automating a process, or creating an autonomous vehicle.

Chapter 2: Introduction to Multi-Agent Systems

In the world of artificial intelligence, individual intelligent agents can perform remarkable tasks. But what happens when you bring multiple agents together, enabling them to collaborate, coordinate, and even compete? The result is a **multi-agent system (MAS)**—a fascinating approach to solving complex problems that no single agent could tackle alone.

2.1 Key Concepts of Multi-Agent Systems

Multi-agent systems (MAS) are more than just a collection of individual intelligent agents. They represent a carefully designed framework where multiple agents interact, communicate, and collaborate within a shared environment to achieve complex objectives. To understand how MAS works, let's break this concept into essential components and explore how these systems operate, the dynamics between agents, and their overall architecture.

A multi-agent system is a group of independent agents that work together in an environment to solve problems or achieve goals. These agents can represent anything—robots, software programs, vehicles, or even humans. What makes MAS unique is that no single agent controls the entire system. Instead, each agent has its own decision-making capabilities and interacts with others to accomplish shared or individual objectives.

Think of MAS as a soccer team. Each player (agent) operates autonomously, has a specific role, and contributes to the team's success. Players communicate, collaborate, and adjust their strategies dynamically based on the game's situation. Similarly, agents in MAS can negotiate, share resources, or divide tasks to improve overall system performance.

Key Characteristics of Multi-Agent Systems

1. Autonomy

Each agent operates independently and makes decisions without relying on a central controller. Autonomy allows agents to adapt to local conditions and take actions based on their specific objectives.

Example

Consider a fleet of delivery drones, where each drone autonomously plans its route based on its location and the destination. Even if one drone fails, the others continue their tasks without disruption.

class Drone:

```
def __init__(self, id, location, destination):
    self.id = id
    self.location = location
    self.destination = destination

def plan_route(self):
    print(f"Drone {self.id}: Planning route
from {self.location} to {self.destination}.")

# Example usage
drone1 = Drone(1, "Warehouse A", "Customer X")
drone2 = Drone(2, "Warehouse B", "Customer Y")

drone1.plan_route()
drone2.plan_route()
```

Each drone independently plans its route, showcasing the autonomy of agents in MAS.

2. Interactivity

Agents in MAS must interact with their environment and other agents. This interaction enables them to share information, coordinate tasks, and make collective decisions.

Example

Let's extend the drone example. What if two drones need to communicate to avoid a collision?

class Drone:

```
def __init__(self, id, location):
    self.id = id
    self.location = location
```

```
    def communicate(self, other_drone):
        print(f"Drone {self.id} to Drone
{other_drone.id}: My location is {self.location}.")
        print(f"Drone {other_drone.id} to Drone
{self.id}: My location is {other_drone.location}.")

# Example usage
drone1 = Drone(1, "Point A")
drone2 = Drone(2, "Point B")

drone1.communicate(drone2)
```

Here, the drones exchange location data to prevent collisions, demonstrating interactivity within MAS.

3. Decentralization

In MAS, there is no single central controller managing the agents. Instead, decisions are distributed among the agents, which increases the system's robustness and scalability.

Example

Imagine a smart grid where each household has its own energy meter (agent). The agents communicate to balance energy usage without relying on a central authority.

4. Collaboration and Competition

Agents in MAS can either collaborate to achieve common goals or compete when resources are limited. This dynamic interaction enables MAS to handle complex scenarios.

Real-World Example

Autonomous vehicles at an intersection must collaborate to avoid collisions while competing for the right of way.

Agent Communication in Multi-Agent Systems

Communication is a critical aspect of MAS. Agents use structured messages to exchange information, negotiate, or request resources. This process typically follows protocols that define how agents should interact.

Message Passing

Message passing is the simplest form of agent communication. Agents send and receive messages containing data or requests.

class Agent:

```
def __init__(self, name):
    self.name = name

def send_message(self, recipient, message):
    print(f"{self.name} to {recipient.name}:
{message}")

def receive_message(self, sender, message):
    print(f"{self.name} received from
{sender.name}: {message}")

# Example usage
agent1 = Agent("Agent A")
agent2 = Agent("Agent B")

agent1.send_message(agent2, "Do you have the
data?")
agent2.receive_message(agent1, "Do you have the
data?")
```

In this example, two agents exchange messages using a basic communication mechanism. In larger systems, communication is often handled through specialized protocols like **Agent Communication Languages (ACL)**.

Emergent Behavior in Multi-Agent Systems

One of the most exciting aspects of MAS is the concept of emergent behavior. When individual agents interact within a system, their combined actions can lead to outcomes that are greater than the sum of their parts. This emergent behavior is not explicitly programmed but arises naturally from the interactions.

Example: Flocking Behavior

Consider a flock of birds. Each bird (agent) follows simple rules: maintain distance from others, align with neighbors, and move toward the average position of the group. These simple interactions create complex, coordinated flight patterns.

Practical Code Example: Simulating MAS

Let's build a simple MAS simulation where agents move on a grid and interact with each other.

import random

class Agent:

```
    def __init__(self, id, grid_size):
        self.id = id
        self.position = (random.randint(0,
grid_size - 1), random.randint(0, grid_size - 1))

    def move(self, grid_size):
        x, y = self.position
        self.position = ((x + random.choice([-1, 0,
1])) % grid_size,
                          (y + random.choice([-1, 0,
1])) % grid_size)
        print(f"Agent {self.id} moved to
{self.position}")

    def communicate(self, other_agent):
        print(f"Agent {self.id} to Agent
{other_agent.id}: My position is {self.position}")

# Example usage
grid_size = 5
agents = [Agent(i, grid_size) for i in range(3)]

# Simulate movements and communication
for _ in range(3):
    for agent in agents:
        agent.move(grid_size)
    agents[0].communicate(agents[1])
```

In this simulation, agents randomly move on a grid and communicate their positions. While basic, it demonstrates the foundation of MAS.

Multi-agent systems are a powerful paradigm for solving complex, distributed problems. By understanding their key concepts— autonomy, interactivity, decentralization, and collaboration—you can design systems that mimic the dynamics of real-world teams or ecosystems. Whether you're managing a fleet of drones, coordinating traffic, or building a smart city, the principles of MAS provide a robust framework for achieving these goals.

2.2 Benefits and Challenges of Multi-Agent Systems

When discussing multi-agent systems (MAS), it's easy to marvel at their capabilities: they can coordinate, solve complex problems, and adapt dynamically to their environment. But just like any sophisticated approach, MAS comes with its own set of strengths and hurdles. To truly understand their potential, it's important to explore both the benefits they bring and the challenges they pose.

Benefits of Multi-Agent Systems

The true power of MAS lies in its ability to harness the collective intelligence of multiple agents. Each agent contributes independently while also being part of a larger system, allowing MAS to excel in areas that require distributed decision-making, flexibility, and robustness.

Distributed Problem-Solving

One of the most significant advantages of MAS is its ability to distribute problem-solving tasks across multiple agents. By breaking down a large problem into smaller, manageable parts, MAS allows each agent to handle specific tasks efficiently. This approach reduces computational overhead and makes the system more scalable.

Example: Disaster Management

In a disaster scenario, MAS can coordinate rescue operations. Imagine a team of autonomous drones deployed to locate survivors in a disaster-stricken area. Each drone focuses on a specific region, scanning for heat signatures or motion. If one drone detects a survivor, it notifies the rest of the system, ensuring a coordinated rescue effort.

Here's a simple code representation of how distributed tasks might be assigned in MAS:

class Drone:

```
    def __init__(self, id, region):
        self.id = id
        self.region = region

    def search(self):
        print(f"Drone {self.id} is searching region
{self.region}")

# Example usage
regions = ["North", "South", "East", "West"]
drones = [Drone(i, region) for i, region in
enumerate(regions, start=1)]

for drone in drones:
    drone.search()
```

Each drone independently handles its assigned region, illustrating how tasks can be distributed in MAS.

Scalability

MAS is inherently scalable because adding new agents to the system doesn't require redesigning the entire system. Instead, new agents integrate seamlessly, enhancing the system's capabilities.

Example: Logistics

In a warehouse, MAS can manage robotic systems to sort and transport packages. If the warehouse expands, additional robots can join the system without disrupting ongoing operations. Each robot works autonomously while communicating with others to avoid collisions and optimize routes.

Robustness and Fault Tolerance

Decentralization makes MAS highly robust. Unlike centralized systems, where the failure of a central controller can cripple the entire system, MAS can continue functioning even if some agents fail. The remaining agents adapt to fill in the gaps, ensuring uninterrupted operations.

Example: Swarm Robotics

In a swarm of drones conducting surveillance, the failure of one drone doesn't affect the others. The remaining drones adjust their coverage to compensate for the loss.

Here's a practical code example that simulates fault tolerance:

class Drone:

```
    def __init__(self, id):
        self.id = id
        self.active = True

    def deactivate(self):
        self.active = False
        print(f"Drone {self.id} is inactive.")

    def operate(self):
        if self.active:
            print(f"Drone {self.id} is
operational.")
        else:
            print(f"Drone {self.id} is offline.")

# Example usage
drones = [Drone(i) for i in range(1, 6)]

# Deactivate one drone
drones[2].deactivate()

# Check the status of all drones
for drone in drones:
    drone.operate()
```

This example shows how the system can identify and adapt to agent failures.

Adaptability to Dynamic Environments

MAS excels in dynamic environments where conditions change frequently. Agents can sense changes in their surroundings and adapt their behavior accordingly, ensuring the system remains effective even in unpredictable scenarios.

Example: Autonomous Traffic Management

In smart cities, MAS can manage traffic lights based on real-time vehicle density. If one intersection experiences high traffic, agents managing nearby intersections can adjust their light cycles to ease congestion.

Challenges of Multi-Agent Systems

While MAS offers remarkable benefits, it also comes with challenges that require careful consideration during design and implementation.

Coordination Complexity

Coordinating multiple agents can be challenging, especially as the system grows. Ensuring agents work together effectively requires robust communication protocols and algorithms. Miscommunication or poor synchronization can lead to inefficiencies or failures.

Example: Drone Fleet Coordination

In a fleet of delivery drones, if one drone doesn't communicate its route properly, it could collide with another or deliver a package to the wrong location.

Here's a simple simulation to illustrate coordination:

class Drone:

```
    def __init__(self, id, route):
        self.id = id
        self.route = route

    def share_route(self):
        return self.route

    def adjust_route(self, new_route):
        self.route = new_route
        print(f"Drone {self.id} adjusted its route
to: {self.route}")
```

```
# Example usage
drone1 = Drone(1, "Route A")
drone2 = Drone(2, "Route B")

# Simulating route sharing
shared_route = drone1.share_route()
drone2.adjust_route(shared_route)
```

This code demonstrates how agents share and adjust information to maintain coordination.

Resource Conflicts

When multiple agents compete for limited resources, conflicts can arise. Resolving these conflicts requires negotiation mechanisms or priority rules.

Example: Resource Allocation in a Factory

If multiple robots need to use the same charging station, a conflict arises. Implementing a queue or priority-based system can help resolve this issue.

Scalability Trade-Offs

While MAS is scalable, adding more agents increases communication overhead. Ensuring efficient communication as the system grows requires optimization strategies, such as hierarchical structures or clustering.

Design and Implementation Costs

Developing MAS is more complex than designing a single-agent system. You must account for agent communication, coordination, fault tolerance, and emergent behaviors, all of which require meticulous planning and testing.

The benefits of MAS—distributed problem-solving, scalability, robustness, and adaptability—make it a powerful tool for addressing complex, dynamic problems. However, challenges like coordination complexity, resource conflicts, and scalability trade-offs highlight the need for thoughtful design and optimization.

By understanding these benefits and challenges, you're better equipped to design MAS that leverages their strengths while mitigating potential pitfalls. This balance is key to unlocking the full potential of multi-agent systems.

2.3 Real-World Applications of Multi-Agent Systems

Multi-agent systems (MAS) are more than just a fascinating concept—they're at the core of many practical and impactful technologies shaping the world today. From logistics and healthcare to autonomous vehicles and financial markets, MAS enables us to solve complex problems by distributing intelligence across multiple agents. In this section, we'll explore several real-world applications of MAS, breaking down their functionality and illustrating how they're implemented.

Logistics and Supply Chain Management

Efficient logistics and supply chain operations are critical in today's global economy. Multi-agent systems play a key role by allowing autonomous agents, such as robots or software modules, to collaborate in managing tasks like inventory tracking, route optimization, and package delivery.

Example: Warehouse Robots

In a modern warehouse, MAS coordinates a fleet of robots that pick, sort, and transport items. Each robot acts as an autonomous agent, making decisions about its route and task priority based on the current workload and its position in the warehouse.

Practical Implementation: Coordinating Warehouse Robots

Here's an example of how MAS can manage multiple robots in a warehouse:

class Robot:

```
def __init__(self, id, position):
    self.id = id
    self.position = position
    self.task = None

def assign_task(self, task):
```

```
        self.task = task
        print(f"Robot {self.id} assigned task:
{self.task}")

    def move_to_position(self, new_position):
        print(f"Robot {self.id} moving from
{self.position} to {new_position}")
        self.position = new_position

# Simulate task allocation
robots = [Robot(i, (0, 0)) for i in range(3)]
tasks = ["Pick item A", "Pick item B", "Deliver to
Zone C"]

for robot, task in zip(robots, tasks):
    robot.assign_task(task)
    robot.move_to_position((2, 3))   # Simulate
movement to task location
```

This example shows how tasks are distributed and executed by robots, demonstrating how MAS can improve efficiency in logistics.

Healthcare Systems

Healthcare is a field that benefits immensely from MAS. Agents in healthcare systems can represent hospitals, doctors, patients, and even medical devices. These agents communicate and collaborate to optimize resource allocation, improve patient care, and manage emergencies.

Example: Emergency Response Coordination

During a pandemic, MAS can coordinate the distribution of medical supplies. Agents representing hospitals communicate their needs, while agents representing suppliers manage inventory and delivery schedules. This ensures that critical resources are distributed efficiently and equitably.

Practical Example: Resource Allocation in Healthcare

Here's a simulation of MAS for distributing medical supplies:

class Hospital:

```python
    def __init__(self, name, demand):
        self.name = name
        self.demand = demand

    def request_supplies(self):
        print(f"{self.name} requests {self.demand}
units of supplies.")

class Supplier:
    def __init__(self, inventory):
        self.inventory = inventory

    def allocate_supplies(self, hospitals):
        for hospital in hospitals:
            allocated = min(hospital.demand,
self.inventory)
            self.inventory -= allocated
            print(f"Allocated {allocated} units to
{hospital.name}. Remaining inventory:
{self.inventory}")

# Example usage
hospitals = [Hospital("Hospital A", 50),
Hospital("Hospital B", 30)]
supplier = Supplier(100)

for hospital in hospitals:
    hospital.request_supplies()

supplier.allocate_supplies(hospitals)
```

This example highlights how agents can dynamically allocate resources based on real-time demands.

Autonomous Vehicles and Traffic Management

One of the most transformative applications of MAS is in autonomous transportation systems. Each vehicle in an MAS is an independent agent that makes decisions about speed, direction, and route. These agents also communicate with one another to avoid collisions, manage traffic flow, and optimize routes.

Example: Intersection Management

In a city with autonomous vehicles, MAS can manage intersections without traffic lights. Vehicles negotiate right-of-way, minimizing wait times and fuel consumption.

Practical Example: Vehicle Communication

Here's how MAS might facilitate communication between autonomous vehicles:

class Vehicle:

```
    def __init__(self, id, position):
        self.id = id
        self.position = position

    def communicate(self, other_vehicle):
        print(f"Vehicle {self.id} to Vehicle
{other_vehicle.id}: My position is
{self.position}.")

    def move(self, new_position):
        print(f"Vehicle {self.id} moving to
{new_position}")
        self.position = new_position

# Example usage
vehicle1 = Vehicle(1, "Intersection A")
vehicle2 = Vehicle(2, "Intersection B")

vehicle1.communicate(vehicle2)
vehicle1.move("Intersection B")
vehicle2.move("Intersection A")
```

This example demonstrates how vehicles coordinate their movements to avoid collisions and ensure smooth traffic flow.

Smart Grids and Energy Distribution

Smart grids use MAS to manage energy generation, distribution, and consumption. Agents in a smart grid represent power plants, substations, and consumers. They work together to balance supply and demand, reduce waste, and optimize energy usage.

Example: Load Balancing

In a smart grid, agents continuously monitor energy usage and redistribute power to areas with higher demand. This prevents outages and ensures efficient use of energy resources.

Financial Markets

Financial markets are another domain where MAS thrives. Agents can represent traders, analyzing market trends and executing trades autonomously. By operating independently yet interacting with one another, these agents contribute to the overall liquidity and stability of the market.

Example: Stock Trading Bots

Trading bots act as agents that monitor stock prices and execute trades based on predefined strategies. They communicate with exchanges and adapt their behavior based on market conditions.

Multi-agent systems are at the heart of many advanced technologies, enabling us to tackle problems that require collaboration, adaptability, and distributed decision-making. From warehouse robots optimizing logistics to autonomous vehicles reshaping transportation, MAS has proven its value across a wide range of industries.

By understanding these real-world applications, you can appreciate how MAS is transforming the way we solve problems and manage resources. As you continue exploring MAS, think about the possibilities for applying these systems to the challenges you face in your own domain.

Chapter 3: Graph Structures in AI

Graphs are everywhere in artificial intelligence, serving as one of the most powerful tools for modeling relationships, processes, and workflows. They enable us to represent complex systems in a way that is both intuitive and computationally efficient. Whether you're analyzing social networks, optimizing supply chains, or building knowledge graphs, understanding graph structures is essential.

This chapter explores the fundamentals of graph theory, how graphs are used to model relationships and workflows in AI, and the role of **LangGraph** in leveraging graph-based approaches for building intelligent agents and multi-agent systems.

3.1 Basics of Graph Theory

Graph theory is a branch of mathematics that provides a way to model relationships, interactions, and connections between entities. It's the foundation for understanding how complex systems are structured and how they operate. Graphs are all around us—they help us understand social networks, optimize delivery routes, model workflows, and much more. If you've ever used a map application to find the shortest path to your destination or seen a recommendation for a new connection on a social media platform, you've interacted with systems that rely on graph theory.

A graph is a collection of **nodes** (also called vertices) and **edges**. Nodes represent entities or objects, and edges represent the relationships or interactions between those entities. Think of a graph as a map where locations are nodes, and roads between them are edges.

Formal Definition

A graph $G=(V,E)$ consists of:

V: A set of nodes or vertices.

E: A set of edges, where each edge connects two nodes.

Example: A Friendship Network

In a social network, nodes represent people, and edges represent friendships. If Alice and Bob are friends, there's an edge between their nodes.

Types of Graphs

Graphs can take various forms depending on their structure and purpose. Here are some key types:

Directed and Undirected Graphs

Directed Graphs (Digraphs): Edges have a direction. For example, in a Twitter network, if Alice follows Bob, there's a directed edge from Alice to Bob.

Undirected Graphs: Edges have no direction. In a Facebook friendship network, if Alice and Bob are friends, there's an undirected edge between them.

Weighted Graphs

Edges can have weights to represent the strength or cost of a relationship. For example, in a road network, weights might represent distances or travel times between cities.

Cyclic and Acyclic Graphs

Cyclic Graphs: Contain at least one loop where you can start at a node and return to it by following edges.

Acyclic Graphs: Contain no loops. Directed Acyclic Graphs (DAGs) are commonly used to represent workflows or task dependencies.

Sparse and Dense Graphs

Sparse Graphs: Have relatively few edges compared to the number of nodes.

Dense Graphs: Have many edges, potentially close to the maximum number.

Graph Representation

To work with graphs programmatically, we need to represent them in a way that computers can process. There are two common representations: **Adjacency Lists** and **Adjacency Matrices**.

Adjacency List

An adjacency list represents the graph as a dictionary where each key is a node, and its value is a list of connected nodes. This is efficient for sparse graphs.

Example: Undirected graph

```
graph = {
    "A": ["B", "C"],
    "B": ["A", "D"],
    "C": ["A", "D"],
    "D": ["B", "C"]
}

# Print neighbors of each node
for node, neighbors in graph.items():
    print(f"{node} is connected to {neighbors}")
```

In this example, node "A" is connected to "B" and "C", forming a simple undirected graph.

Adjacency Matrix

An adjacency matrix represents the graph as a 2D matrix, where rows and columns correspond to nodes. If there's an edge between two nodes, the corresponding cell in the matrix is 1 (or the edge weight); otherwise, it's 0.

```
import numpy as np
```

Example: Directed graph

```
nodes = ["A", "B", "C", "D"]
adj_matrix = np.array([
    [0, 1, 1, 0],    # A -> B, A -> C
    [0, 0, 0, 1],    # B -> D
    [0, 0, 0, 1],    # C -> D
    [0, 0, 0, 0]     # D has no outgoing edges
])

# Print adjacency matrix
print("Adjacency Matrix:")
print(adj_matrix)
```

In this matrix, row ii and column jj indicate whether there's an edge from node ii to node jj.

Graph Properties

Understanding a graph's properties can provide insights into its structure and behavior.

Degree

The degree of a node is the number of edges connected to it. In directed graphs:

In-Degree: Number of incoming edges.

Out-Degree: Number of outgoing edges.

Connectivity

A graph is connected if there's a path between every pair of nodes. In a disconnected graph, some nodes are isolated or form separate subgraphs.

Paths and Cycles

Path: A sequence of edges that connects two nodes.

Cycle: A path that starts and ends at the same node.

Practical Example: Shortest Path in a Graph

Let's compute the shortest path in a weighted graph using Dijkstra's algorithm. This is commonly used in applications like GPS navigation.

```
import heapq

def dijkstra(graph, start):
    # Priority queue for shortest distance
    pq = [(0, start)]   # (distance, node)
    distances = {node: float('inf') for node in
graph}
    distances[start] = 0

    while pq:
```

```python
        current_distance, current_node =
heapq.heappop(pq)

        for neighbor, weight in
graph[current_node]:
            distance = current_distance + weight

            if distance < distances[neighbor]:
                distances[neighbor] = distance
                heapq.heappush(pq, (distance,
neighbor))

    return distances

# Example graph as adjacency list with weights
graph = {
    "A": [("B", 1), ("C", 4)],
    "B": [("C", 2), ("D", 5)],
    "C": [("D", 1)],
    "D": []
}

# Calculate shortest distances from node "A"
shortest_distances = dijkstra(graph, "A")
print("Shortest distances:", shortest_distances)
```

This program calculates the shortest path from node "A" to all other nodes. For example, the shortest path from "A" to "D" is 4 (via "C").

Real-World Applications of Graph Theory

Graphs are incredibly versatile and find applications in diverse fields:

Social Networks: Modeling relationships and interactions between users.

Recommendation Systems: Suggesting items based on user-item interaction graphs.

Transportation Networks: Optimizing routes and managing traffic flow.

Biology: Modeling protein-protein interactions or gene regulatory networks.

Graph theory is a fundamental tool for representing and analyzing relationships, processes, and systems. By understanding its basic concepts—nodes, edges, paths, and connectivity—you can model complex problems effectively. Whether you're building social networks, optimizing workflows, or designing multi-agent systems, the principles of graph theory are invaluable.

3.2 Modeling Relationships and Workflows with Graphs

Graphs are one of the most intuitive and powerful tools to model relationships and workflows. They enable us to represent entities as nodes and their interactions or dependencies as edges. By leveraging graph structures, we can capture complex systems, analyze their behavior, and optimize their performance.

In this section, I'll Walk you through how graphs can be used to model relationships and workflows, using clear examples and code to solidify your understanding. Whether we're building social networks, designing workflows, or creating recommendation systems, graphs provide a clear and structured way to understand these connections.

Modeling Relationships with Graphs

Graphs are ideal for representing relationships between entities. Whether you're working with people in a social network, products in a recommendation system, or cities in a transportation network, graphs let you map out the connections in a clear and computationally efficient way.

Example: Social Networks

In a social network, nodes represent users, and edges represent relationships, such as friendships or followers. Let's create a simple social graph where we model friendships:

```
import networkx as nx
import matplotlib.pyplot as plt

# Create a graph
```

```
social_graph = nx.Graph()

# Add nodes (people)
social_graph.add_nodes_from(["Alice", "Bob",
"Charlie", "Diana", "Eve"])

# Add edges (friendships)
social_graph.add_edges_from([
    ("Alice", "Bob"),
    ("Alice", "Charlie"),
    ("Bob", "Diana"),
    ("Charlie", "Eve"),
    ("Diana", "Eve")
])

# Draw the graph
nx.draw(social_graph, with_labels=True,
node_color='lightblue', font_weight='bold')
plt.show()
```

This example creates a simple undirected graph where edges indicate mutual friendships. The visualization shows how users are connected and helps us analyze the network, such as finding the most connected user or identifying isolated groups.

Analyzing Relationships

Graphs let us answer critical questions about relationships. For instance:

Who has the most connections? This is the node with the highest degree.

What's the shortest path between two people? This identifies how information might flow in a network.

```
# Find the degree of each node (number of
connections)
degrees = dict(social_graph.degree())
print("Node degrees:", degrees)

# Find the shortest path between Alice and Eve
shortest_path = nx.shortest_path(social_graph,
source="Alice", target="Eve")
```

```
print("Shortest path from Alice to Eve:",
shortest_path)
```

This shows us how relationships can be quantified and navigated in a graph structure.

Modeling Workflows with Graphs

Workflows involve a series of tasks or steps, often with dependencies between them. Graphs, particularly Directed Acyclic Graphs (DAGs), are a natural choice for representing workflows because they clearly show how tasks are connected and in what order they should be performed.

Example: Task Dependencies

Let's model a project where tasks depend on each other. For example:

Task A must be completed before Task B and Task C.

Task B and Task C must be completed before Task D.

```
# Create a directed graph (DAG)
workflow_graph = nx.DiGraph()

# Add nodes (tasks)
workflow_graph.add_nodes_from(["Task A", "Task B",
"Task C", "Task D"])

# Add edges (dependencies)
workflow_graph.add_edges_from([
    ("Task A", "Task B"),
    ("Task A", "Task C"),
    ("Task B", "Task D"),
    ("Task C", "Task D")
])

# Draw the workflow graph
nx.draw(workflow_graph, with_labels=True,
node_color='lightgreen', font_weight='bold',
arrows=True)
plt.show()
```

Here, the arrows represent dependencies between tasks. For instance, "Task A → Task B" means Task A must be completed before Task B can start.

Analyzing Workflows

Graphs allow us to analyze workflows to ensure they're efficient and error-free. For instance:

Topological Sorting: Determine the order in which tasks should be performed.

Cycle Detection: Ensure there are no cyclic dependencies, which would prevent task completion.

```
# Find a topological ordering of tasks
task_order =
list(nx.topological_sort(workflow_graph))
print("Task execution order:", task_order)

# Check for cycles in the graph
has_cycle =
nx.is_directed_acyclic_graph(workflow_graph)
print("Does the workflow have cycles?", has_cycle)
```

This ensures that the workflow is valid and provides a clear execution plan.

Practical Applications of Graph-Based Workflows

Let's explore real-world examples where workflows and relationships are modeled using graphs.

Example 1: E-Commerce Order Fulfillment

In an e-commerce warehouse, order fulfillment involves multiple tasks, such as:

Picking items from shelves.

Packing items.

Labeling the package.

Shipping the order.

Each task depends on the previous one. We can model this process as a DAG, where each node is a task and each edge represents a dependency.

```
# Create a directed graph for the e-commerce
workflow
order_fulfillment = nx.DiGraph()

# Define tasks and dependencies
order_fulfillment.add_edges_from([
    ("Pick Items", "Pack Items"),
    ("Pack Items", "Label Package"),
    ("Label Package", "Ship Order")
])

# Visualize the order fulfillment workflow
nx.draw(order_fulfillment, with_labels=True,
node_color='skyblue', font_weight='bold',
arrows=True)
plt.show()
```

This graph ensures that no task is started out of sequence, streamlining the fulfillment process.

Example 2: Transportation Networks

In a transportation system, nodes represent locations (cities or stops), and edges represent routes. Graphs help model the network, optimize routes, and identify bottlenecks.

```
# Define a weighted graph for a transportation
network
transport_graph = nx.Graph()

# Add edges with weights (distances)
transport_graph.add_edges_from([
    ("City A", "City B", {"distance": 5}),
    ("City B", "City C", {"distance": 7}),
    ("City A", "City C", {"distance": 10}),
    ("City C", "City D", {"distance": 3})
])

# Find the shortest path from City A to City D
```

```
shortest_path = nx.shortest_path(transport_graph,
source="City A", target="City D",
weight="distance")
print("Shortest path from City A to City D:",
shortest_path)
```

This example highlights how graphs can optimize travel and reduce costs.

Benefits of Using Graphs for Modeling

Clarity: Graphs provide a clear visual representation of relationships and dependencies.

Scalability: They can handle large, complex systems with ease.

Flexibility: Graphs adapt well to dynamic systems where relationships or tasks change over time.

Graphs are invaluable for modeling relationships and workflows, offering a structured way to represent interactions and dependencies. By using graph structures, you can analyze complex systems, optimize processes, and ensure efficient execution of tasks. Whether you're mapping social connections, managing projects, or designing transportation networks, graphs provide the tools you need to turn abstract problems into actionable solutions.

3.3 The Role of LangGraph in Graph-Based AI

LangGraph is a cutting-edge framework designed specifically to harness the power of graph structures in artificial intelligence. It simplifies the process of building, managing, and scaling intelligent systems by leveraging the natural strengths of graphs. Whether you're designing workflows, modeling relationships, or constructing multi-agent systems, LangGraph provides the tools to create highly adaptable and efficient solutions.

LangGraph is a graph-based framework that enables developers to represent entities and their interactions as nodes and edges in a graph. It provides a structured approach to organizing and executing complex workflows, managing dependencies, and facilitating communication in distributed systems.

At its core, LangGraph offers:

A simple way to define agents, tasks, and relationships.

Tools to dynamically update graphs as systems evolve.

Built-in capabilities for optimizing workflows and analyzing systems.

LangGraph is designed with AI in mind, allowing you to model and manage workflows for machine learning pipelines, multi-agent systems, and knowledge graphs—all within a graph-based architecture.

Why Use LangGraph for AI?

The true strength of LangGraph lies in its ability to bridge the gap between theory and practice. While many tools require you to translate abstract concepts into code manually, LangGraph provides an intuitive framework where you can directly map your ideas into graph-based structures.

Benefits of LangGraph

Visual Clarity: By representing systems as graphs, LangGraph makes workflows and relationships easier to understand and analyze.

Scalability: It handles large and complex systems by allowing nodes and edges to scale dynamically.

Flexibility: LangGraph adapts to changes in your system, such as adding new agents or updating workflows.

Built-in Optimization: It includes algorithms for finding shortest paths, detecting bottlenecks, and balancing resource allocation.

How LangGraph Works

LangGraph uses the principles of graph theory to manage entities (nodes), their relationships (edges), and the rules that govern their interactions. These elements are combined into a graph structure that evolves dynamically as tasks are executed or relationships change.

Key Components

Nodes: Represent agents, tasks, or entities in the system.

Edges: Define relationships or dependencies between nodes.

Attributes: Store metadata for nodes and edges, such as priorities, costs, or statuses.

Rules: Govern how nodes and edges interact, ensuring the system operates smoothly.

Example: Building a Workflow with LangGraph

Let's use LangGraph to model a machine learning pipeline. The pipeline includes the following steps:

Data collection.

Data preprocessing.

Model training.

Model evaluation.

Each step depends on the previous one, making it a perfect fit for LangGraph's directed graph structure.

```python
import networkx as nx
import matplotlib.pyplot as plt

# Define the LangGraph workflow
workflow = nx.DiGraph()

# Add nodes for tasks
workflow.add_nodes_from([
    "Data Collection",
    "Data Preprocessing",
    "Model Training",
    "Model Evaluation"
])

# Define dependencies
workflow.add_edges_from([
    ("Data Collection", "Data Preprocessing"),
    ("Data Preprocessing", "Model Training"),
    ("Model Training", "Model Evaluation")
])

# Visualize the workflow
```

```
nx.draw(workflow, with_labels=True,
node_color='skyblue', font_weight='bold',
arrows=True)
plt.title("Machine Learning Workflow")
plt.show()
```

In this example:

Each node represents a step in the pipeline.

Each edge represents a dependency, ensuring that tasks are executed in the correct order.

Advanced Features of LangGraph

LangGraph doesn't stop at simple workflows. It includes advanced features for more complex systems, such as multi-agent interactions and real-time updates.

Multi-Agent Systems

In multi-agent systems, LangGraph represents agents as nodes and their interactions as edges. It provides tools for managing communication, task allocation, and resource sharing among agents.

Example: Task Allocation in a Multi-Agent System

Consider a system where three agents handle tasks collaboratively. LangGraph helps distribute tasks efficiently based on dependencies and agent capabilities.

```
# Define agents and tasks
agents = ["Agent 1", "Agent 2", "Agent 3"]
tasks = ["Task A", "Task B", "Task C"]

# Create the graph
mas_graph = nx.DiGraph()

# Add agents and tasks as nodes
mas_graph.add_nodes_from(agents + tasks)

# Define task allocations and dependencies
mas_graph.add_edges_from([
    ("Agent 1", "Task A"),
```

```
    ("Agent 2", "Task B"),
    ("Agent 3", "Task C"),
    ("Task A", "Task B"),   # Task A must be
completed before Task B
    ("Task B", "Task C")    # Task B must be
completed before Task C
])

# Visualize the multi-agent system
nx.draw(mas_graph, with_labels=True,
node_color='lightgreen', font_weight='bold',
arrows=True)
plt.title("Multi-Agent Task Allocation")
plt.show()
```

This graph models how agents interact with tasks and each other, ensuring smooth collaboration.

Real-Time Updates

LangGraph allows dynamic changes to the graph structure, making it ideal for systems that evolve over time. For instance:

Adding new agents or tasks to a multi-agent system.

Updating task priorities or dependencies in a workflow.

Reacting to failures, such as reassigning tasks if an agent goes offline.

Example: Adding a New Task

```
# Add a new task and dependency
workflow.add_node("Model Deployment")
workflow.add_edge("Model Evaluation", "Model
Deployment")

# Visualize the updated workflow
nx.draw(workflow, with_labels=True,
node_color='orange', font_weight='bold',
arrows=True)
plt.title("Updated Machine Learning Workflow")
plt.show()
```

This flexibility ensures that LangGraph can adapt to real-world scenarios where systems are rarely static.

Real-World Applications of LangGraph

1. Workflow Automation

LangGraph is widely used to automate complex workflows in industries like healthcare, manufacturing, and software development. For example:

In manufacturing, LangGraph models production line tasks and their dependencies.

In software, it manages CI/CD pipelines, ensuring code is built, tested, and deployed in sequence.

2. Multi-Agent Coordination

LangGraph simplifies the coordination of autonomous agents, such as delivery drones or robotic arms. By representing agents and their tasks in a graph, it optimizes communication and ensures tasks are completed efficiently.

3. Knowledge Graphs

In knowledge management systems, LangGraph helps build and query knowledge graphs, connecting entities like concepts, documents, and metadata.

LangGraph is a powerful tool for building graph-based AI systems, offering clarity, flexibility, and scalability. Whether you're managing workflows, coordinating agents, or modeling relationships, LangGraph provides a structured way to represent and optimize your systems. By embracing LangGraph, you're not just building graphs—you're unlocking the full potential of graph-based AI.

Chapter 4: What is LangGraph?

LangGraph is a purpose-built framework designed to simplify the creation, management, and execution of graph-based systems for artificial intelligence. At its core, LangGraph takes the power of graph theory and applies it to real-world challenges like workflow automation, multi-agent coordination, and knowledge representation. By providing a structured, scalable way to represent nodes (entities) and edges (relationships), LangGraph empowers developers to model and solve complex problems with clarity and efficiency.

4.1 Overview of LangGraph Architecture

LangGraph is a framework designed to simplify the way we model and execute systems using graph-based structures. Its architecture revolves around a few core principles: simplicity, scalability, and adaptability. By integrating the concepts of graph theory with intelligent workflows, LangGraph provides a robust platform for creating dynamic systems that can handle complexity without sacrificing clarity.

The Foundations of LangGraph

At its heart, LangGraph is based on the concept of graphs. In a graph:

Nodes represent entities, such as tasks, agents, or data points.

Edges define relationships or dependencies between these entities.

LangGraph extends this basic graph structure by adding rules, attributes, and workflows, creating a system that can model everything from workflows in a factory to communication in a multi-agent system.

Let's think about why this matters. In a traditional system, relationships between entities are often defined explicitly in code, which can be difficult to adapt as the system grows. LangGraph shifts this paradigm by using graphs as the foundational data structure. This allows relationships to be visualized and modified easily while enabling the system to adapt dynamically.

Core Layers of LangGraph Architecture

LangGraph is designed with modularity in mind, meaning its components are separated into layers that interact seamlessly. This modularity ensures that each part of the system is focused, efficient, and reusable.

1. Graph Layer: The Foundation

The graph layer is the core of LangGraph. It defines the structure of your system: nodes (entities) and edges (relationships). This layer provides:

The ability to add, remove, and modify nodes and edges.

Support for attributes, such as weights, priorities, or statuses.

Code Example: Creating a Graph in LangGraph

Let's start by creating a simple graph with nodes representing tasks and edges representing their dependencies:

```python
import networkx as nx
import matplotlib.pyplot as plt

# Create a directed graph
graph = nx.DiGraph()

# Add nodes (tasks)
graph.add_nodes_from(["Task A", "Task B", "Task
C"])

# Add edges (dependencies)
graph.add_edges_from([
    ("Task A", "Task B"),
    ("Task B", "Task C")
])

# Visualize the graph
nx.draw(graph, with_labels=True,
node_color='lightblue', font_weight='bold',
arrows=True)
plt.title("Basic Task Graph")
plt.show()
```

This simple graph lays the foundation for a workflow. Nodes represent tasks, and edges define the order in which they must be executed.

2. Attribute Layer: Adding Metadata

The attribute layer enhances nodes and edges by allowing you to store metadata. For instance, you might want to assign a status (e.g., "completed", "in progress") to each task or a weight to each edge representing the cost of completing a task.

Code Example: Adding Attributes

Here's how you can add attributes to the graph:

```
# Add attributes to nodes
graph.nodes["Task A"]["status"] = "completed"
graph.nodes["Task B"]["status"] = "in_progress"
graph.nodes["Task C"]["status"] = "pending"

# Add weights to edges
graph["Task A"]["Task B"]["weight"] = 3
graph["Task B"]["Task C"]["weight"] = 5

# Print attributes
for node in graph.nodes(data=True):
    print(f"Node: {node}")

for edge in graph.edges(data=True):
    print(f"Edge: {edge}")
```

Adding attributes provides flexibility, enabling LangGraph to represent systems with greater detail.

3. Rule Layer: Governing Interactions

Rules in LangGraph define how nodes and edges interact. For example:

A rule might enforce that a task can only start once its dependencies are complete.

Another rule could update edge weights dynamically based on system inputs.

Code Example: Defining Rules

Here's how you might enforce a dependency rule:

```
def can_execute(graph, task):
```

```
    """Check if a task can be executed."""
    predecessors = list(graph.predecessors(task))
    for pred in predecessors:
        if graph.nodes[pred]["status"] !=
"completed":
            return False
    return True

# Check if Task B can be executed
if can_execute(graph, "Task B"):
    print("Task B can be executed.")
else:
    print("Task B cannot be executed yet.")
```

This rule ensures that tasks are executed in the correct order, maintaining the integrity of the workflow.

4. Workflow Layer: Orchestrating Processes

The workflow layer combines the graph and rule layers to execute processes. It handles:

Task execution based on dependencies.

Updating the graph dynamically as tasks progress.

Visualizing the state of the workflow in real time.

Code Example: Executing a Workflow

Let's build a simple workflow that processes tasks in order:

```
def execute_workflow(graph):
    """Execute tasks in the workflow."""
    for task in list(graph.nodes):
        if can_execute(graph, task):
            print(f"Executing {task}...")
            graph.nodes[task]["status"] =
"completed"
        else:
            print(f"{task} is waiting for
dependencies.")

# Execute the workflow
```

```
execute_workflow(graph)
```

This script processes tasks in the correct order, updating their statuses as they are executed.

Real-World Applications of LangGraph Architecture

LangGraph's modular architecture makes it ideal for solving real-world problems. Let's look at two examples:

Example 1: Factory Automation

In a factory, LangGraph can model workflows for assembling products:

Nodes represent tasks (e.g., "Cut", "Assemble", "Paint").

Edges represent dependencies between tasks.

Rules ensure tasks are completed in sequence, optimizing efficiency.

Example 2: Multi-Agent Coordination

In a drone delivery system, LangGraph can coordinate routes and tasks:

Nodes represent drones and delivery points.

Edges represent potential routes, weighted by distance or cost.

Rules govern communication between drones to avoid collisions or conflicts.

LangGraph's architecture provides a flexible, scalable, and intuitive way to model and execute complex systems. By combining a robust graph foundation with layers for attributes, rules, and workflows, LangGraph empowers developers to build dynamic, real-world AI applications. Whether you're automating workflows, coordinating agents, or modeling relationships, LangGraph ensures clarity and control at every step.

4.2 Core Components

LangGraph's power lies in its simplicity and structure. At its heart are four core components—**nodes, edges, rules**, and **workflows**—that provide the foundation for modeling and managing complex systems. These components work together seamlessly to represent entities, their relationships, the logic governing their interactions, and the processes that drive them.

Nodes: The Building Blocks

Nodes represent entities within a graph. They could be tasks in a workflow, agents in a multi-agent system, or even physical objects like machines in a factory. Each node is a distinct unit with its own attributes, which can include:

Identifiers: A unique name or ID for the node.

Status: Information about the current state (e.g., "pending", "in progress", "completed").

Metadata: Additional properties, such as priorities, deadlines, or associated resources.

Example: Representing Tasks as Nodes

Let's say we're building a project management tool where tasks are nodes in a graph.

```python
import networkx as nx

# Create a directed graph
project_graph = nx.DiGraph()

# Add nodes with attributes
project_graph.add_node("Task A",
status="completed", priority=1)
project_graph.add_node("Task B",
status="in_progress", priority=2)
project_graph.add_node("Task C", status="pending",
priority=3)

# Display nodes with their attributes
for node, attributes in
project_graph.nodes(data=True):
    print(f"Node: {node}, Attributes:
{attributes}")
```

This simple graph structure lets us keep track of tasks and their associated properties. For example, "Task B" is currently in progress, and its priority is set to 2.

Edges: Connecting the Dots

Edges define relationships between nodes. In LangGraph, edges can represent:

Dependencies: For example, Task A must be completed before Task B.

Communication: For instance, Agent 1 sends a message to Agent 2.

Weights or Costs: Such as the time or resources required to transition between nodes.

Edges can also have attributes, such as weights or conditions, that add depth to the relationships.

Example: Adding Dependencies with Edges

Continuing our project management example, let's add dependencies between tasks.

```
# Add edges with attributes
project_graph.add_edge("Task A", "Task B",
weight=5)
project_graph.add_edge("Task B", "Task C",
weight=3)

# Display edges with their attributes
for edge in project_graph.edges(data=True):
    print(f"Edge: {edge[0]} -> {edge[1]},
Attributes: {edge[2]}")
```

Here, the edge from "Task A" to "Task B" represents a dependency, with a weight of 5 indicating the relative importance or cost of that dependency.

Rules: Governing Interactions

Rules are the logic that defines how nodes and edges interact. They enforce constraints, trigger actions, and ensure that the graph operates according to your system's requirements.

For instance:

A rule might ensure that a task cannot begin until all its dependencies are completed.

Another rule might dynamically update a node's status based on external inputs.

Example: Rule for Task Execution

Let's implement a rule that checks whether a task can be executed based on its dependencies.

```
def can_execute_task(graph, task):
    """Check if all dependencies of a task are
completed."""
    predecessors = list(graph.predecessors(task))
    for dependency in predecessors:
        if graph.nodes[dependency]["status"] !=
"completed":
            return False
    return True

# Check if Task B can be executed
task_to_check = "Task B"
if can_execute_task(project_graph, task_to_check):
    print(f"{task_to_check} can be executed.")
else:
    print(f"{task_to_check} cannot be executed
yet.")
```

In this example, the rule ensures that "Task B" can only start if "Task A" has been completed.

Workflows: Orchestrating Processes

A workflow is a sequence of tasks or operations that follow a specific order. In LangGraph, workflows are represented as directed graphs, with nodes as tasks and edges as dependencies. Workflows are dynamic and can adapt in real time as tasks are completed or conditions change.

Workflows combine nodes, edges, and rules to form a cohesive process. LangGraph provides tools to execute workflows, monitor their progress, and visualize their structure.

Example: Executing a Workflow

Let's create a simple workflow where tasks are executed in order of their dependencies.

```python
def execute_workflow(graph):
    """Execute tasks in the workflow."""
    for task in list(graph.nodes):
        if can_execute_task(graph, task):
            print(f"Executing {task}...")
            graph.nodes[task]["status"] =
"completed"
        else:
            print(f"{task} is waiting for
dependencies.")

# Execute the workflow
execute_workflow(project_graph)

# Display updated node statuses
for node, attributes in
project_graph.nodes(data=True):
    print(f"Node: {node}, Status:
{attributes['status']}")
```

This function processes tasks in the correct order, updating their statuses as they are executed.

Real-World Example: Coordinating a Delivery System

To illustrate how LangGraph's components work together, consider a delivery system with the following requirements:

Drones (nodes) deliver packages (tasks) to locations.

Each package has dependencies, such as picking it up from a warehouse before delivering it.

Rules govern when a drone can move to the next task.

Here's how you can model this system in LangGraph:

```python
# Create a delivery graph
delivery_graph = nx.DiGraph()
```

```
# Add drones and tasks as nodes
delivery_graph.add_nodes_from(["Drone 1", "Task A",
"Task B", "Task C"])

# Add dependencies between tasks
delivery_graph.add_edges_from([
    ("Task A", "Task B"),  # Task A must be
completed before Task B
    ("Task B", "Task C")
])

# Define a rule for drone assignment
def assign_drone_to_task(graph, drone, task):
    if can_execute_task(graph, task):
        print(f"{drone} is assigned to {task}.")
        graph.nodes[task]["status"] = "in_progress"
    else:
        print(f"{task} cannot be started yet.
Waiting for dependencies.")

# Assign Drone 1 to Task A
assign_drone_to_task(delivery_graph, "Drone 1",
"Task A")
```

This system ensures that drones are only assigned to tasks that are ready to be executed, preventing conflicts or delays.

The core components of LangGraph—**nodes**, **edges**, **rules**, and **workflows**—work together to create a powerful framework for modeling and managing complex systems. Nodes represent entities, edges define relationships, rules enforce logic, and workflows bring everything together into dynamic, adaptable processes. By understanding and combining these components, you can design systems that are not only efficient but also resilient to real-world challenges.

Chapter 5: Setting Up LangGraph

To start using LangGraph effectively, it's essential to have a clear understanding of how to set it up, configure it, and integrate it with other AI tools. This chapter will guide you through the installation process, show you how LangGraph interacts seamlessly with popular AI libraries, and introduce you to its APIs, which form the foundation for creating graph-based AI workflows.

5.1 Installation and Configuration

Getting LangGraph up and running on your system is the first step to unlocking its potential. While the process is straightforward, I'll guide you through every detail to ensure you're set up correctly. Along the way, I'll include practical examples and helpful tips to familiarize you with the environment LangGraph operates in.

Step 1: Understanding the Requirements

LangGraph is built to work efficiently in modern programming environments. To ensure compatibility and performance, let's start with what you'll need:

Python 3.8 or later: LangGraph is a Python-based framework, leveraging its versatility and rich ecosystem.

Operating System: LangGraph is cross-platform, so whether you're using Windows, macOS, or Linux, you're good to go.

Package Manager: You'll need pip, Python's default package manager, to install LangGraph and its dependencies.

Before proceeding, ensure Python and pip are installed. You can verify this by running the following commands in your terminal or command prompt:

```
python --version
pip --version
```

If these commands return the version numbers, you're ready to move forward. If not, install Python from python.org.

Step 2: Installing LangGraph

LangGraph is distributed through PyPI, Python's official package repository. Installing it is as simple as running a single command in your terminal:

```
pip install langgraph
```

This command fetches the latest version of LangGraph and its dependencies. The process typically takes just a few seconds.

Verifying the Installation

Once the installation is complete, it's important to confirm that LangGraph is installed correctly. Open a Python shell and type:

```
import langgraph

print("LangGraph version:", langgraph.__version__)
```

If this prints the version number, you're ready to start using LangGraph. If you encounter an error, it may indicate a problem with the installation or your Python environment. In such cases, double-check that you're using the correct version of Python and that your pip is up to date:

```
pip install --upgrade pip
```

Step 3: Basic Configuration

LangGraph is designed to work right out of the box, but it also allows you to customize its behavior to suit your needs. This is particularly useful for debugging, logging, or working with large datasets.

Setting Up Logging

LangGraph includes built-in logging to help you monitor its behavior. By default, it logs important events at the INFO level, but you can increase the verbosity to DEBUG for more detailed insights.

Here's how to configure logging:

```
import langgraph
import logging
```

```
# Configure logging
langgraph.Config.logging_level = "DEBUG"   #
Options: DEBUG, INFO, WARNING, ERROR
logging.basicConfig(level=langgraph.Config.logging_
level)

print("LangGraph logging configured.")
```

This setup ensures that you'll see detailed logs for every operation, which is especially helpful during development and troubleshooting.

Step 4: Creating Your First Graph

To verify that everything is working, let's create a simple graph with LangGraph. We'll start by modeling a small workflow with three tasks, where Task A must be completed before Task B, and Task B before Task C.

```
import langgraph

# Create a LangGraph instance
graph = langgraph.Graph()

# Add nodes (tasks)
graph.add_node("Task A", status="completed")
graph.add_node("Task B", status="pending")
graph.add_node("Task C", status="pending")

# Add edges (dependencies)
graph.add_edge("Task A", "Task B")
graph.add_edge("Task B", "Task C")

# Print the graph structure
print("Nodes in the graph:",
graph.nodes(data=True))
print("Edges in the graph:",
graph.edges(data=True))
```

When you run this code, LangGraph will create a simple directed graph and print its nodes and edges, complete with their attributes. This small exercise confirms that LangGraph is installed and functioning correctly.

Step 5: Handling Common Issues

Even with a straightforward installation process, issues can arise. Here are a few common problems and how to address them:

Issue: ImportError: No module named 'langgraph'

Solution: Ensure LangGraph is installed in the same Python environment you're using. If you're working with virtual environments, activate the correct one before installing LangGraph.

Issue: Permission Denied During Installation

Solution: Use the --user flag to install LangGraph in your user directory:

```
pip install --user langgraph
```

Issue: Compatibility Errors with Dependencies

Solution: Update your dependencies by running:

```
pip install --upgrade langgraph
```

Step 6: Using LangGraph in a Real-World Context

To better understand LangGraph's role, let's apply it to a practical scenario: managing a software development pipeline. This pipeline includes:

Writing code (Task A).

Testing code (Task B).

Deploying code (Task C).

We'll represent these tasks as nodes and their dependencies as edges.

```
# Create the pipeline graph
pipeline = langgraph.Graph()

# Add tasks as nodes
pipeline.add_nodes_from([
```

```
        ("Task A", {"status": "completed"}),
        ("Task B", {"status": "pending"}),
        ("Task C", {"status": "pending"})
])

# Add dependencies as edges
pipeline.add_edges_from([
        ("Task A", "Task B"),
        ("Task B", "Task C")
])

# Print the pipeline structure
print("Pipeline structure:")
print("Nodes:", pipeline.nodes(data=True))
print("Edges:", pipeline.edges(data=True))

# Simulate task execution
def execute_pipeline(graph):
        for node in graph.nodes:
                if all(graph.nodes[dep]["status"] ==
"completed" for dep in graph.predecessors(node)):
                        print(f"Executing {node}...")
                        graph.nodes[node]["status"] =
"completed"
                else:
                        print(f"{node} is waiting for
dependencies.")

execute_pipeline(pipeline)
```

This example demonstrates how LangGraph handles dependencies, making it a perfect tool for orchestrating complex workflows.

Installing and configuring LangGraph is a simple process, but taking the time to understand its setup ensures that you'll be able to use it effectively. By following this guide, you've not only installed LangGraph but also created and managed your first graph. As you move forward, these foundational steps will serve as the basis for leveraging LangGraph in more complex and dynamic applications.

5.2 Integrations with AI Libraries and Tools

LangGraph's real power comes from its ability to integrate seamlessly with the vast ecosystem of AI libraries and tools. Whether you're working with machine learning frameworks, natural language processing libraries, or data visualization tools, LangGraph can complement and enhance your workflows. By representing complex systems as graphs, it bridges the gap between abstract AI workflows and practical implementations.

LangGraph is particularly useful for managing machine learning workflows, where tasks like data preprocessing, model training, and evaluation often depend on one another. Its graph-based approach ensures that workflows are clear, modular, and adaptable.

Example: Managing a Machine Learning Workflow with TensorFlow

Let's say you're building a workflow for training a neural network. The steps include:

Preprocessing data.

Training the model.

Evaluating the model.

We can model this workflow using LangGraph, ensuring each step is executed in the correct order.

```
import langgraph
import tensorflow as tf

# Create a LangGraph instance
workflow = langgraph.Graph()

# Add nodes for each stage
workflow.add_node("Data Preprocessing",
status="pending")
workflow.add_node("Model Training",
status="pending")
workflow.add_node("Model Evaluation",
status="pending")
```

```python
# Define dependencies
workflow.add_edge("Data Preprocessing", "Model
Training")
workflow.add_edge("Model Training", "Model
Evaluation")

# Define functions for each task
def preprocess_data():
    print("Preprocessing data...")
    # Simulate preprocessing
    return
tf.data.Dataset.from_tensor_slices(([[1], [2],
[3]], [1, 0, 1]))

def train_model(data):
    print("Training model...")
    # Simulate model training
    model =
tf.keras.Sequential([tf.keras.layers.Dense(1)])
    model.compile(optimizer='adam',
loss='binary_crossentropy')
    model.fit(data.batch(1), epochs=1)
    return model

def evaluate_model(model):
    print("Evaluating model...")
    # Simulate evaluation
    return model.evaluate([[1], [2], [3]], [1, 0,
1])

# Execute the workflow
data = preprocess_data()
workflow.nodes["Data Preprocessing"]["status"] =
"completed"

if workflow.nodes["Data Preprocessing"]["status"]
== "completed":
    model = train_model(data)
    workflow.nodes["Model Training"]["status"] =
"completed"
```

```
if workflow.nodes["Model Training"]["status"] ==
"completed":
    evaluate_model(model)
    workflow.nodes["Model Evaluation"]["status"] =
"completed"
```

This code combines LangGraph with TensorFlow, creating a robust framework for managing machine learning workflows.

Integrating LangGraph with NetworkX

LangGraph is built on NetworkX, a library that specializes in graph creation and analysis. This makes it easy to leverage NetworkX's powerful algorithms and visualization tools within LangGraph workflows.

Example: Analyzing a Workflow with NetworkX

Suppose you have a workflow for processing orders in an e-commerce platform. You can use NetworkX's built-in algorithms to analyze the workflow and optimize task execution.

```
import networkx as nx

# Create a LangGraph workflow
workflow = nx.DiGraph()

# Add tasks and dependencies
workflow.add_edges_from([
    ("Receive Order", "Process Payment"),
    ("Process Payment", "Pack Items"),
    ("Pack Items", "Ship Order")
])

# Find the execution order using topological sort
execution_order =
list(nx.topological_sort(workflow))
print("Execution order:", execution_order)

# Visualize the workflow
nx.draw(workflow, with_labels=True,
node_color="lightblue", font_weight="bold",
arrows=True)
```

This example demonstrates how LangGraph and NetworkX can work together to analyze and optimize workflows.

Integrating LangGraph with Natural Language Processing (NLP) Libraries

LangGraph is also useful in NLP pipelines, where tasks like tokenization, named entity recognition (NER), and sentiment analysis often depend on one another.

Example: Managing an NLP Pipeline with SpaCy

Here, we'll build an NLP pipeline to:

Tokenize text.

Perform named entity recognition.

Analyze sentiment.

```
import langgraph
import spacy

# Load SpaCy model
nlp = spacy.load("en_core_web_sm")

# Create a LangGraph NLP pipeline
nlp_pipeline = langgraph.Graph()

# Add pipeline stages
nlp_pipeline.add_node("Tokenization",
status="pending")
nlp_pipeline.add_node("Named Entity Recognition",
status="pending")
nlp_pipeline.add_node("Sentiment Analysis",
status="pending")

# Define dependencies
nlp_pipeline.add_edge("Tokenization", "Named Entity
Recognition")
nlp_pipeline.add_edge("Named Entity Recognition",
"Sentiment Analysis")
```

```
# Define tasks
def tokenize(text):
    print("Tokenizing text...")
    doc = nlp(text)
    return [token.text for token in doc]

def named_entity_recognition(text):
    print("Performing NER...")
    doc = nlp(text)
    return [(ent.text, ent.label_) for ent in
doc.ents]

def sentiment_analysis(text):
    print("Analyzing sentiment...")
    # Placeholder for sentiment analysis
    return "Positive"

# Execute the pipeline
text = "Apple is looking at buying U.K. startup for
$1 billion."
tokens = tokenize(text)
nlp_pipeline.nodes["Tokenization"]["status"] =
"completed"

if nlp_pipeline.nodes["Tokenization"]["status"] ==
"completed":
    entities = named_entity_recognition(text)
    nlp_pipeline.nodes["Named Entity
Recognition"]["status"] = "completed"

if nlp_pipeline.nodes["Named Entity
Recognition"]["status"] == "completed":
    sentiment = sentiment_analysis(text)
    nlp_pipeline.nodes["Sentiment
Analysis"]["status"] = "completed"

print("Pipeline executed successfully.")
```

This pipeline models the flow of tasks in an NLP project, ensuring each step is executed sequentially.

Integrating LangGraph with Visualization Tools

Visualization is crucial for understanding workflows and debugging issues. LangGraph integrates seamlessly with libraries like Matplotlib and Plotly for creating intuitive visualizations.

Example: Visualizing a Workflow with Matplotlib

Let's visualize a workflow for building a product prototype.

```python
import matplotlib.pyplot as plt

# Create a workflow
workflow = nx.DiGraph()

# Add tasks and dependencies
workflow.add_edges_from([
    ("Design", "Build Prototype"),
    ("Build Prototype", "Test Prototype"),
    ("Test Prototype", "Launch Product")
])

# Visualize the workflow
nx.draw(workflow, with_labels=True,
node_color="lightgreen", font_weight="bold",
arrows=True)
plt.title("Product Development Workflow")
plt.show()
```

This visualization provides a clear view of the task dependencies, making it easier to track progress.

LangGraph's ability to integrate with AI libraries and tools makes it a versatile framework for a wide range of applications. Whether you're managing machine learning workflows, analyzing systems with NetworkX, or building NLP pipelines, LangGraph enhances your capabilities by providing a structured, graph-based approach. By combining LangGraph with tools like TensorFlow, SpaCy, and Matplotlib, you can create systems that are both powerful and easy to manage.

5.3 Introduction to LangGraph APIs

The LangGraph APIs are the backbone of the framework, providing a set of intuitive and powerful tools to create, manage, and manipulate graph-based workflows. These APIs are designed to help you model complex systems with ease while giving you the flexibility to adapt as your requirements evolve. In this section, we'll walk through the core LangGraph APIs, focusing on their functionality, practical use cases, and step-by-step examples to make each concept clear.

Core Concepts of LangGraph APIs

At its core, LangGraph revolves around three key operations:

Nodes: Representing entities or tasks in your system.

Edges: Defining relationships or dependencies between nodes.

Graph Manipulation: Adding, removing, and modifying nodes and edges, analyzing their structure, and executing workflows.

Let's start by building a mental model of how LangGraph works before diving into code.

1. Working with Nodes

A node is the most basic unit in LangGraph. Nodes can represent anything: tasks in a workflow, agents in a system, or even objects in a simulation. Each node can have attributes like status, priority, or any other metadata you define.

Creating and Managing Nodes

Here's how you can add and manage nodes using LangGraph:

```
import langgraph

# Create a graph instance
graph = langgraph.Graph()

# Add nodes to the graph
graph.add_node("Task A", status="completed",
priority=1)
graph.add_node("Task B", status="in_progress",
priority=2)
graph.add_node("Task C", status="pending",
priority=3)

# Retrieve and display node attributes
```

```
for node in graph.nodes(data=True):
    print(f"Node: {node[0]}, Attributes:
{node[1]}")
```

In this example:

We added three nodes, each with attributes like status and priority.

Using graph.nodes(data=True), we can inspect the nodes and their metadata.

Updating Node Attributes

You can update a node's attributes dynamically:

```
# Update the status of a node
graph.nodes["Task B"]["status"] = "completed"
print("Updated Task B:", graph.nodes["Task B"])
```

This flexibility allows you to modify the graph as the system evolves.

2. Defining Relationships with Edges

Edges in LangGraph define how nodes are connected. They can represent relationships, dependencies, or communication pathways. Each edge can also have attributes like weight, cost, or type.

Adding and Managing Edges

Let's add edges to connect the nodes we created earlier:

```
# Add edges with attributes
graph.add_edge("Task A", "Task B", weight=5)
graph.add_edge("Task B", "Task C", weight=3)

# Retrieve and display edge attributes
for edge in graph.edges(data=True):
    print(f"Edge: {edge[0]} -> {edge[1]},
Attributes: {edge[2]}")
```

In this example:

The edge between "Task A" and "Task B" has a weight of 5, indicating the cost or importance of this relationship.

Analyzing Edges

LangGraph makes it easy to analyze edges and relationships. For instance, you can check if two nodes are connected:

```
# Check if an edge exists
if graph.has_edge("Task A", "Task B"):
    print("Task A is connected to Task B.")
```

3. Graph Manipulation and Analysis

The true power of LangGraph lies in its ability to manipulate and analyze graphs. This includes adding or removing nodes and edges, finding paths, and running graph algorithms.

Removing Nodes and Edges

Here's how you can remove elements from a graph:

```
# Remove a node
graph.remove_node("Task C")
print("Nodes after removal:", list(graph.nodes))

# Remove an edge
graph.remove_edge("Task A", "Task B")
print("Edges after removal:", list(graph.edges))
```

Removing nodes or edges dynamically can help you adapt workflows to changing requirements.

Finding Paths

LangGraph provides built-in methods for finding paths between nodes. For example:

```
# Add edges back for pathfinding
graph.add_edge("Task A", "Task B")
graph.add_edge("Task B", "Task C")

# Find the shortest path
path = graph.shortest_path("Task A", "Task C")
print("Shortest path from Task A to Task C:", path)
```

This functionality is invaluable for optimizing workflows or analyzing dependencies.

4. Executing Workflows

LangGraph's APIs are designed to manage workflows efficiently. You can define tasks, set dependencies, and execute them step by step.

Building and Executing a Workflow

Let's build a simple workflow where tasks are executed in order of their dependencies:

```python
# Define a rule for task execution
def can_execute(graph, task):
    """Check if a task can be executed based on its
dependencies."""
    predecessors = list(graph.predecessors(task))
    for dependency in predecessors:
        if graph.nodes[dependency]["status"] !=
"completed":
            return False
    return True


# Execute the workflow
for task in graph.nodes:
    if can_execute(graph, task):
        print(f"Executing {task}...")
        graph.nodes[task]["status"] = "completed"
    else:
        print(f"{task} is waiting for
dependencies.")
```

This example ensures tasks are executed only when their prerequisites are complete.

5. Advanced Features: Rules and Dynamic Updates

Rules are a unique feature of LangGraph that allow you to enforce constraints or trigger actions. For instance, you might define a rule that prevents tasks from being executed out of order.

Defining Rules

Here's how you can define a custom rule:

```
def enforce_dependency(graph, task):
    """Raise an error if a task is executed without
satisfying dependencies."""
    if not can_execute(graph, task):
        raise ValueError(f"{task} cannot be
executed yet. Dependencies incomplete.")

# Try to execute Task B without completing Task A
try:
    enforce_dependency(graph, "Task B")
except ValueError as e:
    print(e)
```

This ensures that your workflows adhere to defined rules.

6. Visualizing Graphs

Visualization is a key part of working with LangGraph. Its APIs integrate seamlessly with libraries like Matplotlib for creating intuitive visualizations.

Visualizing a Workflow

Here's how you can visualize the workflow we created:

```
import matplotlib.pyplot as plt

# Draw the graph
nx.draw(graph, with_labels=True,
node_color="lightblue", font_weight="bold",
arrows=True)
plt.title("Workflow Visualization")
plt.show()
```

This visualization makes it easy to understand the structure of your workflow at a glance.

Real-World Example: Project Management

To bring everything together, let's model a real-world project management scenario. Imagine a software project with the following tasks:

Writing code (Task A).

Testing code (Task B).

Deploying code (Task C).

```
# Create the project graph
project = langgraph.Graph()

# Add tasks
project.add_node("Write Code", status="completed")
project.add_node("Test Code", status="pending")
project.add_node("Deploy Code", status="pending")

# Add dependencies
project.add_edge("Write Code", "Test Code")
project.add_edge("Test Code", "Deploy Code")

# Execute the project workflow
for task in project.nodes:
    if can_execute(project, task):
        print(f"Executing {task}...")
        project.nodes[task]["status"] = "completed"
    else:
        print(f"{task} is waiting for
dependencies.")
```

This example shows how LangGraph simplifies complex workflows, making them manageable and efficient.

The LangGraph APIs provide a comprehensive toolkit for working with graph-based systems. By mastering these APIs, you can model and manage even the most complex workflows with ease. Whether you're adding nodes, defining rules, or executing workflows, LangGraph gives you the power to create systems that are both efficient and adaptable. As you continue exploring LangGraph, these APIs will become your go-to tools for building intelligent, graph-driven solutions.

Chapter 6: Building Your First Agent in LangGraph

LangGraph empowers you to create intelligent agents that interact, collaborate, and solve complex problems. These agents operate within a graph-based structure, allowing you to model their behavior, relationships, and workflows with clarity and precision. In this chapter, we'll walk through the process of building your first agent in LangGraph, assigning roles, defining goals, and executing basic workflows.

6.1 Step-by-Step Agent Creation

Creating an agent in LangGraph is an intuitive process that combines the principles of graph theory with intelligent system design. In LangGraph, an agent is represented as a node in a graph, enriched with attributes that define its role, goals, and state. Agents interact with their environment and other entities (tasks, data points, or even other agents) via edges, forming a dynamic and scalable system.

Let's build an agent step by step. By the end of this section, you'll have a functional understanding of how to define, configure, and use agents in LangGraph, with practical examples to solidify your understanding.

Step 1: Defining the Graph

The first step in creating an agent is to define the graph where it will operate. This graph serves as the environment, containing both the agent and any tasks or entities it interacts with.

Here's how you create the graph:

```
import langgraph

# Create a LangGraph instance
agent_graph = langgraph.Graph()

# Add an agent node
agent_graph.add_node("Agent 1", role="worker",
status="idle")
print("Agent added:", agent_graph.nodes(data=True))
```

This snippet creates a graph and adds a node for Agent 1. Notice that the node has attributes:

role defines what the agent does.

status reflects the agent's current state (e.g., "idle", "active", "completed").

Step 2: Adding Tasks

Agents typically interact with tasks, which are also represented as nodes. Tasks have attributes such as their status (e.g., "pending", "in progress", "completed") and priority.

Let's add some tasks:

```
# Add task nodes
agent_graph.add_node("Task A", status="pending",
priority=1)
agent_graph.add_node("Task B", status="pending",
priority=2)

# Add edges connecting the agent to its tasks
agent_graph.add_edge("Agent 1", "Task A")
agent_graph.add_edge("Agent 1", "Task B")

# Display the graph structure
print("Graph structure:")
print("Nodes:", agent_graph.nodes(data=True))
print("Edges:", agent_graph.edges(data=True))
```

Here:

The tasks are nodes with their own attributes (status, priority).

The edges represent relationships, connecting the agent to the tasks it can perform.

Step 3: Defining Agent Behavior

Now that the agent and its tasks are defined, let's focus on how the agent behaves. Behavior is determined by rules and functions you define. For example, an agent may check the status of a task before deciding whether to execute it.

Here's a function that simulates an agent executing a task:

```
def execute_task(graph, agent, task):
    """Simulate an agent executing a task."""
    if graph.nodes[task]["status"] == "pending":
        print(f"{agent} is executing {task}...")
        graph.nodes[task]["status"] = "completed"
        graph.nodes[agent]["status"] = "idle"
    else:
        print(f"{task} is already completed.")

Let's put this function to use:
# Execute a task
execute_task(agent_graph, "Agent 1", "Task A")

# Check the updated task status
print("Updated task status:",
agent_graph.nodes["Task A"])
```

In this example:

The agent checks if the task is pending.

If so, it executes the task and updates its own status to "idle" and the task's status to "completed."

Step 4: Adding More Complexity

While the basic structure is functional, real-world agents often deal with more complex scenarios. Let's enhance the agent with additional attributes and functionality.

Assigning a Goal

Goals give the agent direction, helping you define its purpose within the system. For example, an agent's goal might be to complete all tasks it's assigned to.

```
# Assign a goal to the agent
agent_graph.nodes["Agent 1"]["goal"] = "Complete
all assigned tasks"
print("Agent Goal:", agent_graph.nodes["Agent
1"]["goal"])
```

Checking Dependencies

Tasks may depend on other tasks. For instance, Task B can only start after Task A is completed. Let's add this logic:

```
# Add a dependency
agent_graph.add_edge("Task A", "Task B",
dependency=True)

# Define a function to check dependencies
def can_execute_task(graph, task):
    """Check if all dependencies of a task are
completed."""
    predecessors = list(graph.predecessors(task))
    for dep in predecessors:
        if graph.nodes[dep]["status"] !=
"completed":
            return False
    return True

# Check if Task B can be executed
if can_execute_task(agent_graph, "Task B"):
    execute_task(agent_graph, "Agent 1", "Task B")
else:
    print("Task B cannot be executed yet. Waiting
for dependencies.")
```

This ensures that tasks are executed in the correct order, maintaining the integrity of the workflow.

Step 5: Simulating Agent Workflows

Finally, let's simulate a complete workflow where the agent:

Checks its goal.

Identifies pending tasks.

Executes tasks in the correct order.

```
def execute_agent_workflow(graph, agent):
    """Simulate an agent completing its
workflow."""
    print(f"Starting workflow for {agent}...")
```

```
    for task in graph.successors(agent):
        if can_execute_task(graph, task):
            execute_task(graph, agent, task)
        else:
            print(f"{task} is waiting for
dependencies.")
    print(f"{agent} has completed its workflow.")

# Simulate the workflow
execute_agent_workflow(agent_graph, "Agent 1")

# Display the final graph structure
print("Final graph structure:")
print("Nodes:", agent_graph.nodes(data=True))
print("Edges:", agent_graph.edges(data=True))
```

This simulation showcases how an agent can systematically complete tasks, respecting dependencies and updating its state as it works.

Real-World Application: A Delivery Robot

To make things more relatable, consider a delivery robot tasked with moving packages to their destinations. The robot (Agent 1) interacts with packages (Task A, Task B), ensuring each package is delivered in the correct order.

```
# Add package tasks
agent_graph.add_node("Package A", status="pending",
location="Shelf 1")
agent_graph.add_node("Package B", status="pending",
location="Shelf 2")

# Connect the robot to the packages
agent_graph.add_edge("Agent 1", "Package A")
agent_graph.add_edge("Agent 1", "Package B")

# Simulate the delivery workflow
def deliver_packages(graph, agent):
    for package in graph.successors(agent):
        if graph.nodes[package]["status"] ==
"pending":
```

```
          print(f"{agent} is delivering {package}
from {graph.nodes[package]['location']}...")
          graph.nodes[package]["status"] =
"delivered"
        else:
          print(f"{package} is already
delivered.")

deliver_packages(agent_graph, "Agent 1")
```

This simple example mirrors real-world scenarios where agents handle tasks dynamically, making decisions based on the state of their environment.

We've created a functional agent in LangGraph, defined its behavior, and simulated a workflow. These building blocks provide the foundation for more advanced systems, where agents can coordinate, adapt, and solve complex problems. By combining graph structures with intelligent agents, LangGraph opens up endless possibilities for managing dynamic, real-world systems.

6.2 Assigning Roles and Defining Goals

Roles and goals are the backbone of an agent's identity and purpose within a system. In LangGraph, defining roles ensures that agents have specific responsibilities, while setting goals provides them with direction. Together, these attributes transform agents from passive entities into purposeful, task-oriented components capable of driving workflows and solving problems.

A role defines what an agent is designed to do. It outlines the scope of its capabilities and sets boundaries for its interactions. For example:

In a warehouse system, one agent may have the role of a "picker" responsible for gathering items, while another acts as a "packer" for packaging items.

In a software deployment pipeline, roles might include "tester" or "deployer."

Roles are added to agents as attributes, providing context about their purpose within the system.

Defining Roles for Agents

Let's assign a role to an agent using LangGraph:

```python
import langgraph

# Create a LangGraph instance
agent_graph = langgraph.Graph()

# Add an agent with a role
agent_graph.add_node("Agent 1", role="worker",
status="idle")
print(f"Role assigned to Agent 1:
{agent_graph.nodes['Agent 1']['role']}")
```

In this example:

Agent 1 is assigned the role of "worker," indicating that it's responsible for performing tasks.

The role attribute is stored as part of the agent's metadata, making it easily accessible for logic or analysis.

Expanding Roles with Specialization

Roles can be expanded to include specific responsibilities or capabilities. For example, you might define roles like "data_collector" or "analyzer" to differentiate between agents.

```python
# Add specialized roles to agents
agent_graph.add_node("Agent 2",
role="data_collector", status="idle")
agent_graph.add_node("Agent 3", role="analyzer",
status="idle")

# Display roles
for agent, attributes in
agent_graph.nodes(data=True):
    print(f"{agent} has role:
{attributes['role']}")
```

By defining specialized roles, you can create systems where agents collaborate, each contributing based on their expertise.

Setting Goals for Agents

While roles define what an agent is capable of, goals give it direction. A goal answers the question: *What is the agent trying to achieve?* Goals can be simple (e.g., "Complete Task A") or complex (e.g., "Optimize system performance over time").

Assigning Goals to Agents

Goals are typically represented as attributes on agent nodes. Here's how you can assign a goal to an agent:

```
# Assign a goal to Agent 1
agent_graph.nodes["Agent 1"]["goal"] = "Complete
all assigned tasks"

# Display the agent's goal
print(f"Agent 1's goal: {agent_graph.nodes['Agent
1']['goal']}")
```

In this example:

The goal is stored as metadata, making it easy to reference during execution.

Goals can be updated dynamically based on system needs.

Creating Dynamic Goals

Agents often operate in dynamic environments where their goals need to adapt. For example, an agent might reprioritize tasks based on urgency or resource availability.

```
# Dynamically update the goal based on task status
def update_agent_goal(graph, agent):
    pending_tasks = [
        task for task in graph.successors(agent)
        if graph.nodes[task]["status"] == "pending"
    ]
    if pending_tasks:
        graph.nodes[agent]["goal"] = f"Complete
{len(pending_tasks)} pending tasks"
    else:
```

```
        graph.nodes[agent]["goal"] = "All tasks
completed"

# Add tasks to the graph
agent_graph.add_node("Task A", status="pending")
agent_graph.add_node("Task B", status="completed")
agent_graph.add_edge("Agent 1", "Task A")
agent_graph.add_edge("Agent 1", "Task B")

# Update the agent's goal
update_agent_goal(agent_graph, "Agent 1")
print(f"Updated goal for Agent 1:
{agent_graph.nodes['Agent 1']['goal']}")
```

Here, the goal changes based on the number of pending tasks, making the agent more responsive to the system's state.

Practical Example: Roles and Goals in a Delivery System

Let's build a more complex example to see how roles and goals work together in a real-world context. Consider a system where agents represent delivery robots tasked with moving packages.

Defining the System

Robots are agents with the role of "delivery_bot."

Each robot's goal is to deliver its assigned packages.

Packages are tasks, and their status changes as they're picked up and delivered.

```
# Create the graph
delivery_graph = langgraph.Graph()

# Add robots and packages
delivery_graph.add_node("Robot 1",
role="delivery_bot", status="idle", goal="Deliver
assigned packages")
delivery_graph.add_node("Package A",
status="pending", location="Warehouse 1")
delivery_graph.add_node("Package B",
status="pending", location="Warehouse 2")
```

```
# Connect robots to packages
delivery_graph.add_edge("Robot 1", "Package A")
delivery_graph.add_edge("Robot 1", "Package B")

Simulating the Workflow
Now, let's simulate the robot completing its goal.
def execute_delivery(graph, robot):
    """Simulate a robot delivering packages."""
    print(f"{robot} is starting its delivery
workflow...")
    for package in graph.successors(robot):
        if graph.nodes[package]["status"] ==
"pending":
            print(f"{robot} is delivering {package}
from {graph.nodes[package]['location']}...")
            graph.nodes[package]["status"] =
"delivered"
        else:
            print(f"{package} is already
delivered.")
    print(f"{robot} has completed its workflow.")

# Execute the workflow
execute_delivery(delivery_graph, "Robot 1")

# Check the updated statuses
print("Updated statuses:")
for node, attributes in
delivery_graph.nodes(data=True):
    print(f"{node}: {attributes}")
```

In this example:

The robot's role as a "delivery_bot" defines its purpose.

Its goal, "Deliver assigned packages," directs its actions.

The workflow ensures that the robot systematically delivers each package.

Visualization for Better Understanding

To visualize the system and track progress, you can use a graph visualization:

```python
import matplotlib.pyplot as plt

# Visualize the delivery graph
langgraph.visualize(delivery_graph,
with_labels=True, node_color="lightgreen",
font_weight="bold", arrows=True)
plt.title("Delivery System Graph")
plt.show()
```

This visualization helps you see how agents, tasks, and goals are connected, making it easier to debug and optimize the system.

Roles and goals are essential for defining and directing agents in LangGraph. Roles establish what an agent can do, while goals provide the motivation to act. Together, they form the foundation of intelligent, purpose-driven systems. Whether you're managing delivery robots, coordinating tasks in a factory, or designing AI-driven workflows, these concepts ensure that your agents operate effectively and adapt to dynamic environments. By combining roles and goals with LangGraph's graph-based structure, you can build systems that are both intelligent and efficient.

6.3 Executing Basic Workflows

Executing workflows is where the concepts of nodes, edges, roles, and goals come together in LangGraph to create a functioning system. Workflows are the processes that agents follow to accomplish tasks, interact with the environment, and achieve their goals. In this section, I'll guide you through creating, managing, and executing basic workflows using LangGraph, ensuring each step is practical, clear, and immediately useful.

A workflow in LangGraph is a series of interconnected tasks represented as nodes in a graph. The edges between these nodes define the order of execution or dependencies. Agents navigate this workflow, interacting with tasks and updating their states as they progress.

Workflows can be as simple as a linear sequence of tasks or as complex as a dynamic, branching system with multiple agents working in parallel. The beauty of LangGraph is its ability to handle both ends of this spectrum seamlessly.

Setting Up a Basic Workflow

Let's start by creating a basic workflow with three tasks:

Task A must be completed first.

Task B depends on **Task A**.

Task C depends on **Task B**.

Step 1: Defining the Workflow Graph

We begin by creating a graph and adding the tasks as nodes.

```
import langgraph

# Create a graph instance
workflow_graph = langgraph.Graph()

# Add tasks as nodes
workflow_graph.add_node("Task A", status="pending")
workflow_graph.add_node("Task B", status="pending")
workflow_graph.add_node("Task C", status="pending")

# Define dependencies as edges
workflow_graph.add_edge("Task A", "Task B")
workflow_graph.add_edge("Task B", "Task C")

# Display the workflow structure
print("Workflow structure:")
print("Nodes:", workflow_graph.nodes(data=True))
print("Edges:", workflow_graph.edges())
```

Here:

Each task is represented as a node with a status attribute.

The edges define the order in which tasks must be completed.

Step 2: Simulating Task Execution

An agent must execute the tasks in the correct order, respecting their dependencies. Let's define a function that checks dependencies and executes tasks sequentially.

```python
def execute_workflow(graph, agent="Agent 1"):
    """Execute tasks in a workflow graph."""
    print(f"{agent} is starting the workflow...")
    for task in graph.nodes:
        # Check if all predecessors (dependencies)
are completed
        dependencies =
list(graph.predecessors(task))
        if all(graph.nodes[dep]["status"] ==
"completed" for dep in dependencies):
            if graph.nodes[task]["status"] ==
"pending":
                print(f"{agent} is executing
{task}...")
                graph.nodes[task]["status"] =
"completed"
            else:
                print(f"{task} is already
completed.")
        else:
            print(f"{task} is waiting for
dependencies: {dependencies}")

# Execute the workflow
execute_workflow(workflow_graph)

# Display the updated workflow status
print("\nUpdated task statuses:")
for node, attributes in
workflow_graph.nodes(data=True):
    print(f"{node}: {attributes['status']}")
```

This function:

Iterates over each task in the graph.

Checks whether all dependencies of a task are completed.

Executes the task if all its dependencies are satisfied.

Adding Agents to the Workflow

Workflows often involve one or more agents responsible for executing tasks. Let's extend the previous example to include an agent.

Step 1: Assigning an Agent to the Workflow

We'll add an agent as a node and connect it to the tasks it's responsible for.

```
# Add an agent to the graph
workflow_graph.add_node("Agent 1", role="worker",
status="idle")

# Connect the agent to tasks
workflow_graph.add_edge("Agent 1", "Task A")
workflow_graph.add_edge("Agent 1", "Task B")
workflow_graph.add_edge("Agent 1", "Task C")

print("\nGraph structure with agent:")
print("Nodes:", workflow_graph.nodes(data=True))
print("Edges:", workflow_graph.edges())
```

Here, the agent's node is connected to each task, symbolizing its responsibility.

Step 2: Simulating Agent Behavior

Now, we'll simulate the agent executing tasks one by one.

```
def agent_execute_workflow(graph, agent):
    """Simulate an agent executing a workflow."""
    print(f"{agent} is beginning its tasks...")
    for task in graph.successors(agent):
        dependencies =
list(graph.predecessors(task))
        if all(graph.nodes[dep]["status"] ==
"completed" for dep in dependencies):
            if graph.nodes[task]["status"] ==
"pending":
                print(f"{agent} is working on
{task}...")
                graph.nodes[task]["status"] =
"completed"
```

```
                print(f"{task} completed.")
            else:
                print(f"{task} is already
completed.")
        else:
            print(f"{task} cannot start. Waiting
for dependencies: {dependencies}")

# Execute the workflow with the agent
agent_execute_workflow(workflow_graph, "Agent 1")

# Check the updated graph
print("\nFinal task statuses:")
for node, attributes in
workflow_graph.nodes(data=True):
    print(f"{node}: {attributes}")
```

Real-World Example: Software Development Pipeline

To make the concept relatable, let's model a software development pipeline as a workflow:

Code Implementation (Task A)

Code Testing (Task B) depends on Task A.

Code Deployment (Task C) depends on Task B.

Defining the Pipeline

```
# Create the pipeline graph
pipeline_graph = langgraph.Graph()

# Add tasks
pipeline_graph.add_node("Code Implementation",
status="pending")
pipeline_graph.add_node("Code Testing",
status="pending")
pipeline_graph.add_node("Code Deployment",
status="pending")

# Add dependencies
pipeline_graph.add_edge("Code Implementation",
"Code Testing")
```

```
pipeline_graph.add_edge("Code Testing", "Code
Deployment")

# Add a developer as an agent
pipeline_graph.add_node("Developer",
role="engineer", status="idle")
pipeline_graph.add_edge("Developer", "Code
Implementation")
pipeline_graph.add_edge("Developer", "Code
Testing")
pipeline_graph.add_edge("Developer", "Code
Deployment")
```

Simulating the Pipeline Workflow

```
def developer_execute_pipeline(graph, agent):
    """Simulate a developer completing the software
pipeline."""
    print(f"{agent} is starting the development
pipeline...")
    for task in graph.successors(agent):
        dependencies =
list(graph.predecessors(task))
        if all(graph.nodes[dep]["status"] ==
"completed" for dep in dependencies):
            if graph.nodes[task]["status"] ==
"pending":
                print(f"{agent} is working on
{task}...")
                graph.nodes[task]["status"] =
"completed"
                print(f"{task} completed.")
            else:
                print(f"{task} is already
completed.")
        else:
            print(f"{task} cannot start. Waiting
for dependencies: {dependencies}")

# Execute the pipeline
developer_execute_pipeline(pipeline_graph,
"Developer")
```

```
# Display the final pipeline state
print("\nFinal pipeline state:")
for node, attributes in
pipeline_graph.nodes(data=True):
    print(f"{node}: {attributes['status']}")
```

Workflows in LangGraph: Workflows are represented as directed graphs, where tasks are nodes, and dependencies are edges.

Agents and Tasks: Agents interact with tasks by following dependencies and updating statuses dynamically.

Real-World Applications: Whether managing software pipelines, delivery systems, or manufacturing processes, LangGraph workflows are intuitive and scalable.

By mastering these basic workflows, you've taken a significant step toward designing more advanced systems with multiple agents, dynamic task allocation, and real-time updates.

Chapter 7: Designing Multi-Agent Systems

Multi-agent systems are powerful architectures that allow multiple agents to work together, share information, and accomplish tasks that would be impossible for a single agent. LangGraph provides the tools to design, implement, and manage these systems by leveraging graph structures to model agent networks, their interactions, and workflows. In this chapter, we'll explore how to design multi-agent systems by creating networks and hierarchies, enabling inter-agent communication, and managing task allocation while resolving potential conflicts.

7.1 Creating Agent Networks and Hierarchies

Agent networks and hierarchies form the backbone of multi-agent systems. They define how agents interact, collaborate, and organize themselves to achieve complex goals. In LangGraph, creating agent networks involves representing agents as nodes and their relationships as edges. Hierarchies add an additional layer, establishing chains of command or levels of authority among agents. This structure enables seamless collaboration, efficient task allocation, and clear accountability.

An agent network is a graph where:

Nodes represent agents, such as robots, software processes, or teams.

Edges define relationships between agents, such as communication links or collaboration pathways.

Networks can be flat, where all agents are equal, or hierarchical, where some agents oversee or coordinate the activities of others.

Building an Agent Network in LangGraph

Let's start by creating a simple agent network. We'll represent agents and their relationships in a graph.

Step 1: Creating the Graph

First, we create a graph and add agents as nodes. Each agent is characterized by attributes such as role and status.

```
import langgraph

# Create an agent network graph
agent_network = langgraph.Graph()

# Add agents to the network
agent_network.add_node("Agent 1", role="worker",
status="idle")
agent_network.add_node("Agent 2", role="worker",
status="idle")
agent_network.add_node("Agent 3",
role="coordinator", status="active")

# Display the network structure
print("Agent Network:")
print("Nodes:", agent_network.nodes(data=True))
```

In this example:

Agent 1 and Agent 2 are workers, responsible for completing tasks.

Agent 3 is a coordinator, managing the workers.

Step 2: Defining Relationships

Next, we define relationships between agents. These relationships are represented as edges in the graph.

```
# Define relationships
agent_network.add_edge("Agent 1", "Agent 2",
relationship="collaborates_with")
agent_network.add_edge("Agent 3", "Agent 1",
relationship="oversees")
agent_network.add_edge("Agent 3", "Agent 2",
relationship="oversees")

# Display relationships
print("\nRelationships:")
for edge in agent_network.edges(data=True):
    print(f"{edge[0]} -> {edge[1]}:
{edge[2]['relationship']}")
```

Here:

Agent 1 and Agent 2 collaborate on tasks.

Agent 3 oversees both workers, ensuring coordination.

Designing Hierarchies

Hierarchies establish chains of command, ensuring that decision-making and task allocation follow a clear structure. In LangGraph, hierarchical relationships are modeled using directed edges, where the direction indicates authority or control.

Adding a Supervisor to the Network

Let's expand our network by adding a supervisor who oversees the coordinator:

```
# Add a supervisor
agent_network.add_node("Agent 4",
role="supervisor", status="active")

# Define hierarchical relationships
agent_network.add_edge("Agent 4", "Agent 3",
relationship="supervises")

# Display the updated hierarchy
print("\nUpdated Hierarchy:")
for edge in agent_network.edges(data=True):
    print(f"{edge[0]} -> {edge[1]}:
{edge[2]['relationship']}")
```

In this hierarchy:

Agent 4 supervises Agent 3, ensuring that the coordinator manages the workers effectively.

Simulating Agent Interactions

A network is only useful if the agents can interact meaningfully. Let's simulate a simple scenario where the supervisor sends instructions to the coordinator, and the coordinator allocates tasks to the workers.

```
# Simulate a message from the supervisor to the
coordinator
agent_network["Agent 4"]["Agent 3"]["message"] =
"Ensure tasks are completed on time."

# Simulate task allocation by the coordinator
agent_network["Agent 3"]["Agent 1"]["message"] =
"Complete Task A."
agent_network["Agent 3"]["Agent 2"]["message"] =
"Complete Task B."

# Display messages
print("\nMessages:")
for edge in agent_network.edges(data=True):
    if "message" in edge[2]:
        print(f"Message from {edge[0]} to
{edge[1]}: {edge[2]['message']}")
```

This example demonstrates how information flows through the hierarchy:

The supervisor issues high-level instructions.

The coordinator translates these instructions into actionable tasks for the workers.

Real-World Example: Warehouse Management System

Let's apply these concepts to a real-world scenario—a warehouse management system. In this system:

Supervisors oversee operations.

Coordinators manage specific sections of the warehouse.

Workers (robots) handle tasks like picking and packing items.

Defining the Warehouse Network

```
# Create the warehouse network
warehouse_network = langgraph.Graph()

# Add agents
warehouse_network.add_node("Supervisor",
role="supervisor", status="active")
```

```
warehouse_network.add_node("Coordinator A",
role="coordinator", status="active")
warehouse_network.add_node("Robot 1",
role="picker", status="idle")
warehouse_network.add_node("Robot 2",
role="packer", status="idle")

# Define hierarchical relationships
warehouse_network.add_edge("Supervisor",
"Coordinator A", relationship="supervises")
warehouse_network.add_edge("Coordinator A", "Robot
1", relationship="manages")
warehouse_network.add_edge("Coordinator A", "Robot
2", relationship="manages")
```

Simulating Task Allocation

Now, let's simulate the flow of tasks in the warehouse:

```
# Add tasks
tasks = {
    "Pick Item A": {"status": "pending"},
    "Pack Item A": {"status": "pending"},
}

# Allocate tasks through the hierarchy
def allocate_task(network, coordinator, robot,
task):
    """Simulate task allocation."""
    if tasks[task]["status"] == "pending":
        tasks[task]["status"] = "assigned"
        print(f"{coordinator} instructs {robot} to
{task}.")
        network[coordinator][robot]["task"] = task
    else:
        print(f"{task} is already assigned.")

# Allocate tasks
allocate_task(warehouse_network, "Coordinator A",
"Robot 1", "Pick Item A")
allocate_task(warehouse_network, "Coordinator A",
"Robot 2", "Pack Item A")
```

This example demonstrates:

How tasks flow through the hierarchy from the coordinator to the robots.

The use of graph attributes to store task-related metadata.

Visualizing the Network

To better understand the structure of the agent network, let's visualize it:

```
import matplotlib.pyplot as plt

# Visualize the warehouse network
langgraph.visualize(warehouse_network,
with_labels=True, node_color="lightblue",
font_weight="bold", arrows=True)
plt.title("Warehouse Management Network")
plt.show()
```

This visualization shows the hierarchy and relationships between agents, providing clarity on how the system is organized.

Agent Networks: These represent the relationships between agents, enabling collaboration and communication.

Hierarchies: Establishing chains of command ensures clear accountability and efficient task allocation.

Practical Applications: From warehouses to software development pipelines, agent networks and hierarchies provide a scalable framework for managing complex systems.

By designing agent networks and hierarchies in LangGraph, you can build systems that are both organized and adaptable, ready to tackle real-world challenges with precision and efficiency.

7.2 Inter-Agent Communication and Collaboration

In a multi-agent system, communication and collaboration are the lifeblood of coordinated activity. Agents don't work in isolation; they exchange information, share resources, and work together to accomplish goals. Whether they're robots in a warehouse, software services in a distributed system, or autonomous vehicles in a fleet, agents rely on communication to coordinate their actions and resolve conflicts.

Communication in multi-agent systems involves the exchange of messages between agents. These messages can include:

Instructions: Commands from one agent to another.

Status Updates: Information about an agent's current state or progress.

Resource Requests: Requests for data, tools, or assistance.

In LangGraph, communication is modeled using **edges** and their **attributes**. Edges represent the communication pathways, while attributes store the content and context of the communication.

Setting Up a Communication Network

Let's start by creating a network of agents that can exchange messages.

Step 1: Defining the Network

We'll create a graph with three agents: a manager and two workers.

```
import langgraph

# Create a communication network graph
communication_network = langgraph.Graph()

# Add agents to the network
communication_network.add_node("Manager",
role="manager", status="active")
communication_network.add_node("Worker 1",
role="worker", status="idle")
```

```
communication_network.add_node("Worker 2",
role="worker", status="idle")

# Define communication pathways
communication_network.add_edge("Manager", "Worker
1", channel="instruction")
communication_network.add_edge("Manager", "Worker
2", channel="instruction")
communication_network.add_edge("Worker 1", "Worker
2", channel="collaboration")

# Display the network structure
print("Communication Network:")
print("Nodes:",
communication_network.nodes(data=True))
print("Edges:",
communication_network.edges(data=True))
```

In this setup:

The **manager** communicates instructions to the workers.

The workers can collaborate directly with each other.

Step 2: Sending Messages

To simulate communication, we'll use edge attributes to store messages exchanged between agents.

```
# Send messages through the network
communication_network["Manager"]["Worker
1"]["message"] = "Start Task A."
communication_network["Manager"]["Worker
2"]["message"] = "Start Task B."
communication_network["Worker 1"]["Worker
2"]["message"] = "Need help with Task A."

# Display messages
print("\nMessages:")
for edge in communication_network.edges(data=True):
    if "message" in edge[2]:
        print(f"Message from {edge[0]} to
{edge[1]}: {edge[2]['message']}")
```

Here, each message is stored as an attribute on the edge, making it easy to access and update.

Designing Collaborative Workflows

Collaboration occurs when agents work together to complete a shared task. This requires communication to coordinate their actions and resolve dependencies.

Example: Completing a Shared Task

Let's simulate a scenario where two workers collaborate on a task.

```
# Define a shared task
shared_task = {"Task A": {"status": "pending",
"progress": 0}}

# Function for collaboration
def collaborate_on_task(graph, task, agent1,
agent2):
    """Simulate two agents collaborating on a
task."""
    if task["status"] == "pending":
        print(f"{agent1} and {agent2} are
collaborating on the task.")
        task["progress"] += 50
        if task["progress"] >= 100:
            task["status"] = "completed"
            print(f"{task} completed.")
        else:
            print(f"{task} is still in progress:
{task['progress']}% completed.")
    else:
        print(f"{task} is already completed.")

# Simulate collaboration
collaborate_on_task(communication_network,
shared_task["Task A"], "Worker 1", "Worker 2")
```

This example demonstrates how two agents can work together, updating the task's progress as they collaborate.

Conflict Resolution During Collaboration

Conflicts can arise when multiple agents attempt to claim the same resource or task. LangGraph allows you to implement conflict resolution mechanisms using rules and priorities.

Example: Resolving Task Conflicts

Let's simulate a conflict where two workers attempt to claim the same task.

```
# Define tasks
tasks = {
    "Task B": {"status": "pending", "assigned_to":
None}
}

# Function to resolve conflicts
def resolve_task_conflict(task, agent1, agent2):
    """Resolve conflict when two agents attempt the
same task."""
    if task["assigned_to"] is None:
        task["assigned_to"] = agent1
        print(f"Conflict resolved: {agent1}
assigned to the task.")
    else:
        print(f"Conflict detected: Task already
assigned to {task['assigned_to']}.")
        print(f"{agent2} will wait or request a
different task.")

# Simulate a conflict
resolve_task_conflict(tasks["Task B"], "Worker 1",
"Worker 2")
```

This mechanism ensures that conflicts are resolved efficiently without disrupting the workflow.

Real-World Example: Disaster Response System

To bring these concepts to life, let's model a disaster response system where agents collaborate to deliver supplies and rescue individuals.

System Overview

Drones (Agents) deliver supplies to affected areas.

Teams (Agents) coordinate rescues.

Communication is essential to avoid resource duplication and ensure efficient operations.

Defining the System

```
# Create the disaster response graph
disaster_response = langgraph.Graph()

# Add agents
disaster_response.add_node("Drone 1",
role="supply_delivery", status="idle")
disaster_response.add_node("Drone 2",
role="supply_delivery", status="idle")
disaster_response.add_node("Team 1", role="rescue",
status="active")

# Define communication pathways
disaster_response.add_edge("Drone 1", "Team 1",
channel="status_update")
disaster_response.add_edge("Drone 2", "Team 1",
channel="status_update")
disaster_response.add_edge("Drone 1", "Drone 2",
channel="coordination")

# Display the network structure
print("Disaster Response System:")
print("Nodes:", disaster_response.nodes(data=True))
print("Edges:", disaster_response.edges(data=True))

Simulating Communication
# Send messages
disaster_response["Drone 1"]["Team 1"]["message"] =
"Supplies delivered to Zone A."
disaster_response["Drone 2"]["Team 1"]["message"] =
"En route to Zone B."
disaster_response["Drone 1"]["Drone 2"]["message"]
= "Zone A cleared, proceed to Zone B."

# Display messages
print("\nDisaster Response Messages:")
```

```
for edge in disaster_response.edges(data=True):
    if "message" in edge[2]:
        print(f"Message from {edge[0]} to
{edge[1]}: {edge[2]['message']}")
```

This example highlights how agents coordinate to deliver supplies and manage rescues in a dynamic environment.

Communication Pathways: Use edges and attributes to model the flow of information between agents.

Collaboration: Simulate agents working together to achieve shared goals, updating tasks dynamically.

Conflict Resolution: Implement rules to manage resource contention and ensure smooth operations.

By mastering inter-agent communication and collaboration in LangGraph, you can design systems that are not only efficient but also resilient to real-world challenges. These principles are fundamental for building scalable, multi-agent architectures in diverse applications.

7.3 Task Allocation and Conflict Resolution

Efficient task allocation and conflict resolution are cornerstones of a well-functioning multi-agent system. In LangGraph, these processes are naturally modeled using graph structures. Task allocation involves assigning tasks to the most suitable agents, while conflict resolution ensures that agents do not overlap on the same task or resource, preventing inefficiency and chaos.

Task allocation refers to distributing tasks among agents based on their roles, availability, and capabilities. This ensures that work is completed efficiently and resources are used effectively.

Step 1: Setting Up the System

Let's start by creating a graph to represent agents and tasks. Each task will be a node with attributes such as status and priority, and agents will be connected to tasks they are eligible to perform.

```
import langgraph

# Create a task allocation graph
```

```
task_graph = langgraph.Graph()

# Add agents
task_graph.add_node("Agent 1", role="picker",
status="idle")
task_graph.add_node("Agent 2", role="packer",
status="idle")

# Add tasks
task_graph.add_node("Task A", status="pending",
priority=1)
task_graph.add_node("Task B", status="pending",
priority=2)

# Connect agents to tasks
task_graph.add_edge("Agent 1", "Task A",
eligibility="yes")
task_graph.add_edge("Agent 2", "Task B",
eligibility="yes")

# Display the graph structure
print("Task Allocation Graph:")
print("Nodes:", task_graph.nodes(data=True))
print("Edges:", task_graph.edges(data=True))
```

In this graph:

Agents are connected to tasks they can perform.

Task attributes such as priority help determine which tasks are more urgent.

Step 2: Allocating Tasks Dynamically

Dynamic task allocation involves assigning tasks to agents based on current conditions, such as their availability or the task's urgency.

```
# Define a function for task allocation
def allocate_task(graph, agent, task):
    """Assign a task to an agent if it is
pending."""
    if graph.nodes[task]["status"] == "pending":
        graph.nodes[task]["status"] = "assigned"
```

```
        graph.nodes[task]["assigned_to"] = agent
        graph.nodes[agent]["status"] = "busy"
        print(f"{task} assigned to {agent}.")
    else:
        print(f"{task} is not available for
assignment.")

# Allocate tasks
allocate_task(task_graph, "Agent 1", "Task A")
allocate_task(task_graph, "Agent 2", "Task B")

# Check updated task statuses
print("\nUpdated Task Statuses:")
for node, attributes in
task_graph.nodes(data=True):
    if "status" in attributes:
        print(f"{node}: {attributes['status']}")
```

This code ensures that tasks are only assigned if they are still pending, and updates both the task and agent statuses.

Conflict Resolution in Multi-Agent Systems

Conflicts arise when multiple agents try to claim the same task or resource. Resolving these conflicts efficiently is essential to maintaining a smooth workflow.

Step 1: Detecting Conflicts

Conflicts occur when a task is simultaneously requested by multiple agents. LangGraph makes it easy to detect conflicts by checking the connections between agents and tasks.

```
# Simulate a conflict where two agents want the
same task
task_graph.add_edge("Agent 1", "Task B",
eligibility="yes")

# Detect conflicts
def detect_conflict(graph, task):
    """Check for conflicts on a task."""
    contenders = [
        agent for agent in graph.predecessors(task)
```

```
        if graph[agent][task]["eligibility"] ==
"yes"
    ]
    if len(contenders) > 1:
        print(f"Conflict detected for {task}.
Contenders: {', '.join(contenders)}")
        return contenders
    else:
        print(f"No conflict for {task}.")
        return None

# Detect conflict for Task B
conflict_agents = detect_conflict(task_graph, "Task
B")
```

In this example, the system identifies that both Agent 1 and Agent 2 are eligible for Task B.

Step 2: Resolving Conflicts

Conflicts can be resolved using various strategies, such as prioritizing agents based on their role, availability, or previous workload.

```
# Resolve conflicts by prioritizing based on agent
roles
def resolve_conflict(graph, task, contenders):
    """Resolve task conflict by prioritizing
agents."""
    for agent in contenders:
        if graph.nodes[agent]["role"] == "packer":
            graph.nodes[task]["status"] =
"assigned"
            graph.nodes[task]["assigned_to"] =
agent
            graph.nodes[agent]["status"] = "busy"
            print(f"Conflict resolved: {task}
assigned to {agent}.")
            return
    print(f"Conflict could not be resolved for
{task}.")

# Resolve conflict for Task B
if conflict_agents:
```

```
    resolve_conflict(task_graph, "Task B",
conflict_agents)
```

Here:

The system assigns the task to the agent with the role of packer.

If no priority criteria are met, the conflict remains unresolved.

Real-World Example: Factory Automation

To make these concepts concrete, let's model a factory automation system where robots allocate and complete tasks like assembling and packaging products.

System Overview

Robots (agents) are responsible for different stages of production.

Tasks like assembly and packaging are dynamically assigned.

Conflicts are resolved based on task priority.

Implementation

```
# Create the factory graph
factory_graph = langgraph.Graph()

# Add robots
factory_graph.add_node("Robot 1", role="assembler",
status="idle")
factory_graph.add_node("Robot 2", role="packer",
status="idle")

# Add tasks
factory_graph.add_node("Assemble Product",
status="pending", priority=2)
factory_graph.add_node("Package Product",
status="pending", priority=1)

# Define eligibility
factory_graph.add_edge("Robot 1", "Assemble
Product", eligibility="yes")
factory_graph.add_edge("Robot 2", "Package
Product", eligibility="yes")
```

```
# Simulate task allocation
allocate_task(factory_graph, "Robot 1", "Assemble
Product")
allocate_task(factory_graph, "Robot 2", "Package
Product")

# Simulate a conflict
factory_graph.add_edge("Robot 1", "Package
Product", eligibility="yes")
conflict_agents = detect_conflict(factory_graph,
"Package Product")
if conflict_agents:
    resolve_conflict(factory_graph, "Package
Product", conflict_agents)
```

Visualization for Better Understanding

To visualize the task allocation process, use LangGraph's visualization tools:

```
import matplotlib.pyplot as plt

# Visualize the factory graph
langgraph.visualize(factory_graph,
with_labels=True, node_color="lightblue",
font_weight="bold", arrows=True)
plt.title("Factory Automation Graph")
plt.show()
```

This visualization highlights the relationships between agents and tasks, making it easier to identify bottlenecks and conflicts.

Key Points

Dynamic Task Allocation: Assign tasks to agents based on their roles, availability, and task priorities.

Conflict Detection and Resolution: Use graph analysis to identify and resolve conflicts, ensuring smooth workflows.

Real-World Applications: From factories to disaster response, task allocation and conflict resolution are essential for managing multi-agent systems.

By mastering these principles in LangGraph, you can design intelligent systems that are both efficient and adaptive, capable of handling the complexities of real-world operations.

Chapter 8: Advanced Techniques in LangGraph

LangGraph is a versatile framework that enables you to go beyond basic workflows and agent management, venturing into more sophisticated territory where artificial intelligence and large-scale systems converge. In this chapter, we'll explore how to integrate machine learning and natural language processing, apply reinforcement learning to create adaptive systems, and scale LangGraph for distributed environments. These advanced techniques will empower you to design highly intelligent, scalable, and efficient systems.

8.1 Integrating Machine Learning and NLP

Integrating machine learning (ML) and natural language processing (NLP) into LangGraph unlocks a new level of intelligence for agents and workflows. By leveraging these technologies, you can create systems capable of making data-driven decisions, processing human language, and dynamically adapting to complex scenarios. This section will guide you through integrating ML and NLP with LangGraph, with detailed examples and clear explanations to ensure a comprehensive understanding.

Why Integrate ML and NLP with LangGraph?

LangGraph provides a robust framework for modeling workflows and interactions, while ML and NLP add layers of intelligence. For example:

Machine learning models can predict task priorities, estimate resources, or optimize workflows based on historical data.

NLP models allow agents to interpret and act on human language, bridging the gap between users and systems.

By combining these capabilities, you create agents that are not only task-oriented but also context-aware and adaptive.

Integrating Machine Learning with LangGraph

Let's start by incorporating a machine learning model into a LangGraph workflow. A common use case is task prioritization, where a model predicts the importance of tasks based on their features.

Step 1: Setting Up the Workflow

First, we create a graph representing a set of tasks, each with attributes such as urgency, complexity, and estimated time to complete.

```
import langgraph
import numpy as np
from sklearn.ensemble import RandomForestClassifier

# Create a LangGraph instance
workflow = langgraph.Graph()

# Add tasks with features for priority prediction
workflow.add_node("Task A", features=[1, 0, 5],
priority=None)
workflow.add_node("Task B", features=[0, 1, 3],
priority=None)

print("Workflow tasks:")
for node, data in workflow.nodes(data=True):
    print(f"{node}: Features = {data['features']}")
```

Step 2: Training a Machine Learning Model

We'll use a simple machine learning model to predict task priorities. For this example, we use scikit-learn to train a Random Forest classifier.

```
# Training data
X_train = np.array([
    [1, 0, 5],   # Task with high urgency
    [0, 1, 3],   # Task with high complexity
    [1, 1, 4],   # Task with balanced features
])
y_train = np.array([1, 2, 1])   # Priorities: 1 =
High, 2 = Low

# Train the model
model = RandomForestClassifier()
model.fit(X_train, y_train)
print("\nMachine learning model trained.")
```

Step 3: Using the Model in the Workflow

We use the trained model to predict priorities for each task in the workflow.

```
# Predict task priorities
for node in workflow.nodes:
    features = workflow.nodes[node]["features"]
    priority = model.predict([features])[0]
    workflow.nodes[node]["priority"] = priority
    print(f"{node} assigned priority: {priority}")
```

This integration allows you to automatically prioritize tasks based on their attributes, enabling agents to focus on high-priority tasks first.

Integrating NLP with LangGraph

Natural language processing enables agents to understand and act on human language inputs. This is particularly useful for tasks like extracting instructions from text, responding to user queries, or summarizing workflows.

Step 1: Extracting Tasks from Text

Let's use SpaCy, a popular NLP library, to extract tasks from a natural language description.

```
import spacy

# Load an NLP model
nlp = spacy.load("en_core_web_sm")

# Example text describing tasks
text = "The robot should clean the living room and
organize the storage area."

# Extract tasks using named entity recognition
doc = nlp(text)
tasks = [chunk.text for chunk in doc.noun_chunks]
print("\nExtracted tasks:", tasks)
```

Here, the system identifies potential tasks from the user's description, such as "clean the living room" and "organize the storage area."

Step 2: Adding Extracted Tasks to the Workflow

Once tasks are extracted, they can be added to the LangGraph workflow.

```
# Add extracted tasks to the workflow
for task in tasks:
    workflow.add_node(task, status="pending",
priority=None)

print("\nUpdated workflow nodes:")
for node, data in workflow.nodes(data=True):
    print(f"{node}: {data}")
```

Now the workflow includes tasks derived from natural language input, ready for agents to process.

Step 3: Generating Responses Using NLP

NLP can also generate natural language responses, helping agents communicate with users.

```
# Generate a response for task confirmation
def confirm_tasks(tasks):
    task_list = ", ".join(tasks)
    return f"Tasks added to the workflow:
{task_list}."

response = confirm_tasks(tasks)
print("\nResponse:", response)
```

This approach ensures that the system remains user-friendly, providing feedback in natural language.

Real-World Application: Intelligent Task Manager

To illustrate the integration of ML and NLP, consider an intelligent task manager that:

Receives tasks via voice or text input.

Extracts and prioritizes tasks using NLP and ML.

Allocates tasks dynamically to agents.

Implementation

```python
# Simulated task input
task_input = "Prepare the presentation, clean the
office, and schedule a meeting."

# NLP to extract tasks
doc = nlp(task_input)
tasks = [chunk.text for chunk in doc.noun_chunks]

# Add tasks to workflow with placeholder features
for task in tasks:
    workflow.add_node(task, features=[1, 0, 3],
priority=None)

# Use ML to prioritize tasks
for node in workflow.nodes:
    features = workflow.nodes[node]["features"]
    priority = model.predict([features])[0]
    workflow.nodes[node]["priority"] = priority

# Display prioritized tasks
print("\nPrioritized tasks:")
for node, data in workflow.nodes(data=True):
    print(f"{node}: Priority = {data['priority']}")
```

Key Benefits of ML and NLP Integration

Automation: Automatically prioritize and allocate tasks using machine learning.

Natural Interaction: Enable agents to understand and respond to human language.

Adaptability: Build systems that adapt to dynamic inputs and changing priorities.

By integrating machine learning and NLP with LangGraph, you transform workflows into intelligent, responsive systems capable of handling real-world complexities. This combination not only enhances efficiency but also makes your systems more intuitive and user-friendly.

8.2 Reinforcement Learning for Adaptive Systems

Reinforcement learning (RL) is a cornerstone of adaptive systems. It allows agents to learn optimal behaviors by interacting with their environment and receiving feedback in the form of rewards. Unlike traditional supervised learning, where the agent learns from labeled data, RL focuses on learning through trial and error, making it ideal for dynamic and complex scenarios where rules or outcomes are not explicitly defined.

Reinforcement learning is based on the following core concepts:

Agent: The decision-maker (e.g., a robot, software process, or virtual assistant).

Environment: The system the agent interacts with (e.g., a graph representing workflows or tasks).

Action: The choices the agent makes at each step (e.g., allocating a task or moving to a node).

Reward: Feedback the agent receives after performing an action (e.g., positive for successful task completion, negative for failure).

Policy: The strategy the agent follows to decide its actions (learned over time).

Applying Reinforcement Learning in LangGraph

LangGraph is an excellent framework for implementing reinforcement learning because it provides a natural way to model environments, agents, and workflows.

Step 1: Defining the Environment

The environment in RL is the system where the agent operates. Let's define a simple task allocation system where an agent selects tasks to maximize rewards.

```
import langgraph
import random

# Create a graph to represent tasks and rewards
task_graph = langgraph.Graph()
```

```python
# Add tasks with rewards
task_graph.add_node("Task A", reward=10,
status="pending")
task_graph.add_node("Task B", reward=5,
status="pending")
task_graph.add_node("Task C", reward=20,
status="pending")

# Add an agent node
task_graph.add_node("Agent", role="learner",
total_reward=0)

# Connect the agent to tasks
task_graph.add_edge("Agent", "Task A")
task_graph.add_edge("Agent", "Task B")
task_graph.add_edge("Agent", "Task C")

# Display the environment
print("Environment:")
for node, data in task_graph.nodes(data=True):
    print(f"{node}: {data}")
```

Here:

Tasks are represented as nodes with attributes like reward and status.

The agent interacts with tasks through edges.

Step 2: Defining the Reward System

The reward system provides feedback to the agent after each action. Positive rewards encourage desired behavior, while negative rewards discourage undesirable actions.

```python
# Function to calculate reward
def get_reward(graph, task):
    """Return the reward for completing a task."""
    if graph.nodes[task]["status"] == "pending":
        return graph.nodes[task]["reward"]
    else:
        return -10  # Penalty for attempting an
already completed task
```

Step 3: Implementing the Learning Process

We'll implement a basic reinforcement learning loop where the agent selects tasks, receives rewards, and updates its total reward.

```
# RL learning process
def reinforcement_learning(graph, agent,
episodes=5):
    """Simulate reinforcement learning for task
allocation."""
    for episode in range(episodes):
        print(f"\nEpisode {episode + 1}")
        # Randomly select a task
        task =
random.choice(list(graph.successors(agent)))
        reward = get_reward(graph, task)

        # Update agent's total reward
        graph.nodes[agent]["total_reward"] +=
reward

        # Update task status if completed
        if reward > 0:
            graph.nodes[task]["status"] =
"completed"
            print(f"{agent} completed {task} and
received a reward of {reward}.")
        else:
            print(f"{agent} attempted {task} but
received a penalty of {reward}.")

        print(f"Total reward:
{graph.nodes[agent]['total_reward']}")

# Train the agent
reinforcement_learning(task_graph, "Agent")
```

In this example:

The agent explores the environment by selecting tasks randomly.

Rewards guide the agent's actions, incentivizing task completion.

Advanced RL: Q-Learning for Optimal Policy

Q-learning is a popular RL algorithm that helps agents learn an optimal policy. It maintains a Q-table where each entry represents the expected reward of taking an action in a particular state.

Implementing Q-Learning

Let's implement Q-learning for task allocation.

```
import numpy as np

# Initialize Q-table
tasks = ["Task A", "Task B", "Task C"]
q_table = {task: 0 for task in tasks}   # Q-values
initialized to 0
learning_rate = 0.1
discount_factor = 0.9
episodes = 10

# Q-learning process
for episode in range(episodes):
    print(f"\nEpisode {episode + 1}")
    task = random.choice(tasks)

    # Get reward and update Q-value
    reward = get_reward(task_graph, task)
    max_future_q = max(q_table.values())
    q_table[task] = q_table[task] + learning_rate *
(reward + discount_factor * max_future_q -
q_table[task])

    # Update task status if completed
    if reward > 0:
        task_graph.nodes[task]["status"] =
"completed"
    print(f"Q-values: {q_table}")
```

In this implementation:

The agent updates its Q-values after each episode, learning which tasks yield higher rewards over time.

The Q-table represents the agent's knowledge of the environment.

Real-World Example: Adaptive Delivery System

Let's apply RL to an adaptive delivery system where drones (agents) deliver packages to maximize efficiency.

Defining the System

Drones select delivery zones based on expected rewards (e.g., time saved, customer satisfaction).

Each zone has a reward value that depends on factors like delivery distance or urgency.

```
# Create a delivery system graph
delivery_system = langgraph.Graph()

# Add zones with rewards
delivery_system.add_node("Zone A", reward=15,
status="pending")
delivery_system.add_node("Zone B", reward=10,
status="pending")
delivery_system.add_node("Zone C", reward=5,
status="pending")

# Add a drone
delivery_system.add_node("Drone 1", total_reward=0)

# Connect the drone to zones
delivery_system.add_edge("Drone 1", "Zone A")
delivery_system.add_edge("Drone 1", "Zone B")
delivery_system.add_edge("Drone 1", "Zone C")

# Reinforcement learning for delivery
reinforcement_learning(delivery_system, "Drone 1")
```

This example demonstrates how drones can learn to prioritize zones that maximize rewards, improving delivery efficiency over time.

Learning Through Interaction: RL enables agents to adapt by interacting with their environment and learning from feedback.

Reward-Driven Optimization: Rewards incentivize agents to make decisions that maximize efficiency or minimize costs.

Scalable Applications: From task allocation to autonomous vehicles, RL enhances system adaptability in dynamic scenarios.

By integrating reinforcement learning into LangGraph, you can create intelligent, adaptive systems that evolve over time, learning to optimize workflows, handle uncertainties, and achieve better outcomes.

8.3 Distributed Systems and Scalability

As systems grow in complexity, scalability becomes essential. Distributed systems, which operate across multiple machines or nodes, are the key to handling large-scale workloads efficiently. LangGraph, with its graph-based architecture, provides a natural framework for modeling and managing distributed systems. By partitioning workflows, distributing tasks, and enabling inter-node communication, LangGraph helps you design scalable systems that can adapt to increasing demands.

Distributed systems allow you to:

Scale workloads across multiple nodes or machines.

Enhance reliability by reducing single points of failure.

Increase efficiency through parallel processing and optimized resource usage.

LangGraph's flexibility makes it a powerful tool for representing distributed environments, enabling you to visualize, simulate, and manage these systems.

Modeling Distributed Systems in LangGraph

In LangGraph, distributed systems can be modeled as graphs where:

Nodes represent physical or logical entities (e.g., servers, agents, or tasks).

Edges define communication or resource-sharing pathways.

Step 1: Defining the Distributed Environment

Let's start by creating a distributed system graph with multiple servers and tasks.

```python
import langgraph

# Create a graph for the distributed system
distributed_system = langgraph.Graph()

# Add servers (nodes)
distributed_system.add_node("Server 1",
capacity=100, status="active")
distributed_system.add_node("Server 2",
capacity=150, status="active")
distributed_system.add_node("Server 3",
capacity=200, status="active")

# Add tasks
distributed_system.add_node("Task A", size=50,
status="pending")
distributed_system.add_node("Task B", size=75,
status="pending")
distributed_system.add_node("Task C", size=120,
status="pending")

# Connect servers to tasks
distributed_system.add_edge("Server 1", "Task A",
bandwidth=1000)
distributed_system.add_edge("Server 2", "Task B",
bandwidth=800)
distributed_system.add_edge("Server 3", "Task C",
bandwidth=1200)

# Display the graph
print("Distributed System Structure:")
for node, data in
distributed_system.nodes(data=True):
    print(f"{node}: {data}")
```

In this example:

Servers have attributes like capacity to define their processing capabilities.

Tasks are connected to servers with edges that represent communication bandwidth.

Graph Partitioning for Scalability

When a graph becomes too large to handle on a single machine, partitioning it into smaller subgraphs can improve performance and manageability.

Step 2: Partitioning the Graph

Partitioning involves dividing the graph into smaller, independent subgraphs that can be processed in parallel.

```
import networkx as nx

# Convert LangGraph to NetworkX graph for
partitioning
nx_graph =
nx.convert_node_labels_to_integers(distributed_syst
em)

# Partition the graph into subgraphs
subgraphs = list(nx.connected_components(nx_graph))
partitioned_graphs = [nx_graph.subgraph(nodes) for
nodes in subgraphs]

print("\nPartitioned Subgraphs:")
for i, subgraph in enumerate(partitioned_graphs):
    print(f"Subgraph {i + 1}: Nodes =
{subgraph.nodes}")
```

Here:

The system is divided into smaller components based on connectivity.

Each subgraph can be processed independently, enabling distributed execution.

Distributing Workloads

Once the graph is partitioned, workloads can be distributed across multiple servers. LangGraph facilitates this by enabling you to assign tasks based on server capacity and task size.

Step 3: Task Allocation in Distributed Systems

Let's implement a function to distribute tasks across servers based on their capacities.

```
# Task allocation function
def allocate_task_to_server(graph, task, servers):
    """Allocate a task to the most suitable
server."""
    for server in servers:
        if graph.nodes[server]["capacity"] >=
graph.nodes[task]["size"]:
            graph.nodes[task]["status"] =
"assigned"
            graph.nodes[server]["capacity"] -=
graph.nodes[task]["size"]
            print(f"{task} allocated to {server}.
Remaining capacity:
{graph.nodes[server]['capacity']}")
            return
    print(f"No server has enough capacity for
{task}.")

# Allocate tasks
servers = ["Server 1", "Server 2", "Server 3"]
allocate_task_to_server(distributed_system, "Task
A", servers)
allocate_task_to_server(distributed_system, "Task
B", servers)
allocate_task_to_server(distributed_system, "Task
C", servers)
```

This function ensures:

Tasks are assigned to servers with sufficient capacity.

Server capacity is updated dynamically.

Communication in Distributed Systems

Efficient communication between nodes is crucial for distributed systems. LangGraph models communication pathways using edges, allowing you to simulate data flow and bandwidth constraints.

Simulating Communication

Let's simulate data transfer between servers.

```
# Simulate data transfer
def simulate_data_transfer(graph, source,
destination, data_size):
    """Simulate data transfer between servers."""
    if graph.has_edge(source, destination):
        bandwidth = graph.edges[source,
destination]["bandwidth"]
        transfer_time = data_size / bandwidth
        print(f"Transferring {data_size} units of
data from {source} to {destination}...")
        print(f"Estimated transfer time:
{transfer_time:.2f} seconds.")
    else:
        print(f"No direct connection between
{source} and {destination}.")

# Simulate a transfer
simulate_data_transfer(distributed_system, "Server
1", "Task A", 50)
```

This simulation calculates the transfer time based on data size and bandwidth, providing insights into system performance.

Real-World Example: Content Delivery Network (CDN)

A content delivery network (CDN) is a distributed system designed to deliver content (e.g., videos, files) to users efficiently. Let's model a simplified CDN using LangGraph.

Defining the CDN

```
# Create the CDN graph
cdn = langgraph.Graph()

# Add edge servers
cdn.add_node("Edge Server 1", capacity=500,
location="North America")
cdn.add_node("Edge Server 2", capacity=300,
location="Europe")
```

```
cdn.add_node("Edge Server 3", capacity=400,
location="Asia")

# Add content
cdn.add_node("Video A", size=200, popularity=80)
cdn.add_node("Video B", size=150, popularity=60)

# Connect servers to content
cdn.add_edge("Edge Server 1", "Video A",
bandwidth=1000)
cdn.add_edge("Edge Server 2", "Video B",
bandwidth=800)
cdn.add_edge("Edge Server 3", "Video A",
bandwidth=1200)
```

Simulating Content Delivery

```
# Simulate content delivery
def deliver_content(graph, server, content):
    """Simulate content delivery from a server."""
    if graph.nodes[server]["capacity"] >=
graph.nodes[content]["size"]:
        graph.nodes[server]["capacity"] -=
graph.nodes[content]["size"]
        print(f"{content} delivered from {server}.
Remaining capacity:
{graph.nodes[server]['capacity']}")
    else:
        print(f"{server} does not have enough
capacity for {content}.")

# Deliver content
deliver_content(cdn, "Edge Server 1", "Video A")
deliver_content(cdn, "Edge Server 2", "Video B")
```

This model demonstrates how LangGraph can represent and simulate a CDN, optimizing content delivery based on server capacities and bandwidth.

Scaling Distributed Systems

Scaling a distributed system involves adding more nodes or optimizing resource allocation. LangGraph supports dynamic graph updates, allowing you to model system growth.

Adding Nodes Dynamically

```
# Add a new server dynamically
cdn.add_node("Edge Server 4", capacity=600,
location="South America")
cdn.add_edge("Edge Server 4", "Video A",
bandwidth=900)
print("\nUpdated CDN Structure:")
print("Nodes:", cdn.nodes(data=True))
```

This flexibility ensures that your system can scale as demands increase.

Graph Partitioning: Divide large graphs into smaller subgraphs to enable parallel processing and scalability.

Task Distribution: Dynamically allocate tasks to nodes based on capacity and workload.

Communication Simulation: Model data flow and bandwidth constraints to optimize inter-node communication.

Real-World Applications: From CDNs to distributed databases, LangGraph helps design scalable, efficient systems.

LangGraph provides a comprehensive framework for building and managing distributed systems, empowering you to handle scalability challenges with precision and efficiency. By modeling your systems as graphs, you gain clarity, flexibility, and the tools to adapt to real-world demands.

Chapter 9: Specialized Use Cases

LangGraph's versatility makes it suitable for an array of specialized applications, from automating workflows to conducting multi-agent simulations for research and planning. In this chapter, we'll explore how LangGraph can be tailored for workflow optimization, used to simulate and analyze complex systems, and applied to specific industries like healthcare, logistics, and finance. By the end, you'll have a clear understanding of how LangGraph's features translate into real-world impact across various domains.

9.1 Workflow Automation and Optimization

Workflow automation and optimization are critical for improving efficiency, reducing costs, and minimizing errors in any system. By using LangGraph, you can model workflows as graphs, enabling a clear visualization of tasks, dependencies, and potential bottlenecks. Automation ensures that workflows progress smoothly without manual intervention, while optimization focuses on streamlining the process to achieve better outcomes with fewer resources.

At its core, a workflow is a series of tasks connected by dependencies. These tasks may involve sequential or parallel execution, and their progression depends on specific conditions. LangGraph represents workflows as directed graphs, where:

Nodes are tasks or processes.

Edges define dependencies or relationships between tasks.

Setting Up a Basic Workflow

Let's create a simple workflow for processing customer orders in an online store. The workflow includes:

Receiving the order.

Processing the payment.

Preparing the package.

Shipping the order.

```
import langgraph
```

```
# Create a workflow graph
workflow = langgraph.Graph()

# Add tasks
workflow.add_node("Receive Order",
status="pending", duration=1)
workflow.add_node("Process Payment",
status="pending", duration=2)
workflow.add_node("Prepare Package",
status="pending", duration=3)
workflow.add_node("Ship Order", status="pending",
duration=1)

# Define dependencies between tasks
workflow.add_edge("Receive Order", "Process
Payment")
workflow.add_edge("Process Payment", "Prepare
Package")
workflow.add_edge("Prepare Package", "Ship Order")

# Display the workflow structure
print("Workflow Tasks:")
for node, data in workflow.nodes(data=True):
    print(f"{node}: {data}")
```

This graph clearly shows the sequential nature of the workflow and the dependencies between tasks.

Automating the Workflow

Automation ensures that tasks progress without manual intervention. In LangGraph, you can define rules to control when a task is executed based on the status of its dependencies.

Implementing Automation

```
# Function to execute the workflow
def execute_workflow(graph):
    """Automate task execution based on
dependencies."""
    print("\nExecuting Workflow:")
    for node in list(graph.nodes):
        # Check if all dependencies are completed
```

```
            dependencies =
list(graph.predecessors(node))
        if all(graph.nodes[dep]["status"] ==
"completed" for dep in dependencies):
            if graph.nodes[node]["status"] ==
"pending":
                # Simulate task execution
                graph.nodes[node]["status"] =
"completed"
                print(f"{node} executed.")

# Execute the workflow
execute_workflow(workflow)

# Display the updated workflow status
print("\nUpdated Task Statuses:")
for node, data in workflow.nodes(data=True):
    print(f"{node}: {data['status']}")
```

This function:

Iterates through each task in the graph.

Checks if all dependencies of a task are marked as completed.

Marks the task as completed if its dependencies are satisfied.

Optimizing the Workflow

Optimization involves reducing processing time, minimizing costs, or improving resource utilization. LangGraph supports various optimization techniques, such as identifying bottlenecks and applying critical path analysis.

Identifying Bottlenecks

A bottleneck is a task that slows down the entire workflow. Bottlenecks can be identified by analyzing task durations and dependencies.

```
# Identify the longest task
longest_task = max(workflow.nodes, key=lambda node:
workflow.nodes[node]["duration"])
```

```
print(f"\nBottleneck Task: {longest_task} with
duration
{workflow.nodes[longest_task]['duration']}")
```

By identifying the task with the longest duration, you can focus your optimization efforts where they are needed most.

Applying Critical Path Analysis

The critical path is the longest sequence of tasks that determines the total time required to complete the workflow. LangGraph integrates with NetworkX for advanced graph analysis, including critical path detection.

```
import networkx as nx

# Convert LangGraph to NetworkX graph for analysis
nx_workflow =
nx.convert_node_labels_to_integers(workflow)

# Find the critical path
critical_path = nx.dag_longest_path(nx_workflow,
weight="duration")
print(f"\nCritical Path: {critical_path}")
```

This analysis highlights the sequence of tasks that directly impacts the total workflow duration. Reducing the time of tasks on the critical path will shorten the overall process.

Real-World Application: Manufacturing Workflow

Let's apply these concepts to a manufacturing scenario where products are assembled, inspected, and packaged.

Modeling the Workflow

```
# Create a manufacturing workflow
manufacturing = langgraph.Graph()

# Add tasks
manufacturing.add_node("Assemble Components",
status="pending", duration=5)
```

```
manufacturing.add_node("Quality Inspection",
status="pending", duration=3)
manufacturing.add_node("Packaging",
status="pending", duration=2)

# Define dependencies
manufacturing.add_edge("Assemble Components",
"Quality Inspection")
manufacturing.add_edge("Quality Inspection",
"Packaging")

# Display the workflow
print("\nManufacturing Workflow:")
for node, data in manufacturing.nodes(data=True):
    print(f"{node}: {data}")
```

Optimizing the Manufacturing Workflow

Parallelizing Tasks: Check if tasks can be executed concurrently to reduce total duration.

```
# Parallelize tasks
manufacturing.add_node("Documentation",
status="pending", duration=1)
manufacturing.add_edge("Assemble Components",
"Documentation")
```

Resource Allocation: Assign workers or machines to tasks based on capacity and workload.

```
# Simulate resource allocation
resources = {"Worker A": "Assemble Components",
"Worker B": "Quality Inspection"}
for worker, task in resources.items():
    print(f"{worker} assigned to {task}.")
```

Visualizing the Workflow

Visualization helps in understanding the structure and dependencies of the workflow.

```
import matplotlib.pyplot as plt

# Visualize the workflow
```

```
nx.draw(nx_workflow, with_labels=True,
node_color="lightblue", font_weight="bold",
arrows=True)
plt.title("Workflow Visualization")
plt.show()
```

This visualization provides a clear picture of the workflow, making it easier to identify areas for improvement.

Automation: LangGraph enables the seamless execution of workflows by automating task progression based on dependencies.

Optimization: Techniques like critical path analysis and bottleneck identification help streamline workflows for efficiency.

Real-World Applications: From e-commerce to manufacturing, workflow automation and optimization save time, reduce costs, and improve outcomes.

By applying these principles with LangGraph, you can build systems that are not only efficient but also adaptable to dynamic requirements, ensuring long-term success in any operational environment.

9.2 Multi-Agent Simulations for Research and Planning

Multi-agent simulations are powerful tools for understanding complex systems, testing scenarios, and planning strategies. By representing agents as nodes in a graph and their interactions as edges, LangGraph provides an intuitive framework for creating simulations. These simulations are useful across various domains, from urban planning to disaster response, helping researchers and decision-makers make informed choices.

A multi-agent simulation involves multiple autonomous entities, or agents, interacting within a shared environment. Each agent has:

Attributes that define its state (e.g., location, role, or status).

Behaviors governed by rules or algorithms (e.g., moving toward a goal or reacting to stimuli).

Interactions with other agents or the environment (e.g., collaboration or competition).

By modeling these elements in LangGraph, you can simulate and analyze complex systems in a structured, flexible manner.

Building a Multi-Agent Simulation in LangGraph

Let's create a simple evacuation simulation where agents represent individuals navigating a building to reach an exit.

Step 1: Defining the Environment

The environment is modeled as a graph, where nodes represent locations (e.g., rooms, exits), and edges represent pathways between them.

```
import langgraph

# Create the simulation graph
simulation = langgraph.Graph()

# Add locations (nodes)
simulation.add_node("Room A", type="room",
capacity=5)
simulation.add_node("Room B", type="room",
capacity=5)
simulation.add_node("Exit", type="exit",
capacity=100)

# Add pathways (edges)
simulation.add_edge("Room A", "Room B", distance=3)
simulation.add_edge("Room B", "Exit", distance=2)
simulation.add_edge("Room A", "Exit", distance=5)

# Display the environment
print("Simulation Environment:")
for node, data in simulation.nodes(data=True):
    print(f"{node}: {data}")
```

Here:

Rooms are locations where agents can reside.

Pathways have attributes like distance, representing the cost or time to traverse.

Step 2: Adding Agents

Agents are represented as nodes with attributes like their location and status.

```
# Add agents
simulation.add_node("Agent 1", type="agent",
location="Room A", status="active")
simulation.add_node("Agent 2", type="agent",
location="Room B", status="active")

# Connect agents to their initial locations
simulation.add_edge("Agent 1", "Room A")
simulation.add_edge("Agent 2", "Room B")

# Display agents
print("\nAgents in Simulation:")
for node, data in simulation.nodes(data=True):
    if data["type"] == "agent":
        print(f"{node}: {data}")
```

Each agent has a location attribute, which updates dynamically during the simulation.

Simulating Agent Behavior

Agents in a simulation follow predefined rules. For example, in an evacuation scenario, agents move toward the exit, minimizing their travel distance.

Step 3: Implementing Agent Movement

Let's define a function to simulate agent movement based on the shortest path to the exit.

```
import networkx as nx

# Convert LangGraph to NetworkX for pathfinding
nx_simulation =
nx.convert_node_labels_to_integers(simulation)
```

```python
# Simulate agent movement
def move_agent(graph, agent, destination):
    """Move an agent toward the destination."""
    current_location =
graph.nodes[agent]["location"]
    path = nx.shortest_path(nx_simulation,
source=current_location, target=destination,
weight="distance")

    if len(path) > 1:
        next_location = path[1]   # Move to the next
step in the path
        graph.nodes[agent]["location"] =
next_location
        print(f"{agent} moved from
{current_location} to {next_location}.")
    else:
        print(f"{agent} has reached the
destination: {destination}.")

# Move Agent 1 toward the Exit
move_agent(simulation, "Agent 1", "Exit")
```

This function uses **shortest path algorithms** to calculate the optimal route for each agent.

Step 4: Handling Interactions

Agents may interact with each other or the environment during the simulation. For example, if multiple agents try to enter a room, the room's capacity may limit their access.

```python
# Simulate room capacity checks
def check_room_capacity(graph, room, agent):
    """Ensure the room has capacity for the
agent."""
    current_occupancy = len([n for n, d in
graph.nodes(data=True) if d.get("location") ==
room])
    room_capacity = graph.nodes[room]["capacity"]

    if current_occupancy < room_capacity:
        print(f"{agent} entered {room}.")
```

```
    else:
        print(f"{agent} could not enter {room} due
to capacity limits.")

# Check capacity for Room B
check_room_capacity(simulation, "Room B", "Agent
1")
```

This ensures that the simulation accounts for environmental constraints, creating realistic scenarios.

Advanced Simulations: Collaborative Agents

Some scenarios involve collaboration, where agents work together to achieve a common goal. For example, in a search-and-rescue operation, agents may share information about hazards or locate survivors.

Example: Collaborative Search

Add a hazard and a survivor to the environment

```
simulation.add_node("Hazard", type="hazard",
location="Room B")
simulation.add_node("Survivor", type="survivor",
location="Room A")

# Define collaboration behavior
def collaborate(graph, agent1, agent2):
    """Simulate collaboration between two
agents."""
    if graph.nodes[agent1]["location"] ==
graph.nodes[agent2]["location"]:
        print(f"{agent1} and {agent2} are
collaborating in
{graph.nodes[agent1]['location']}.")

# Simulate collaboration
collaborate(simulation, "Agent 1", "Agent 2")
```

This model demonstrates how agents can exchange information or work together based on their proximity or shared objectives.

Real-World Applications of Multi-Agent Simulations

1. Urban Planning

In urban planning, simulations can model pedestrian flow, traffic patterns, or public transportation systems. For example:

Agents represent individuals or vehicles.

Nodes represent intersections, stations, or destinations.

By simulating scenarios like rush hour traffic or emergency evacuations, planners can optimize infrastructure and resources.

2. Disaster Response

Simulations help plan disaster response strategies by modeling the behavior of first responders, evacuees, and affected areas. For instance:

Agents prioritize rescuing survivors or delivering supplies.

The environment includes hazards, blocked pathways, and safe zones.

3. Social Behavior Research

Simulations are also valuable for studying group dynamics, resource sharing, or conflict resolution. For example:

Agents represent individuals in a community.

Their interactions provide insights into cooperation, competition, or collective decision-making.

Multi-Agent Dynamics: LangGraph allows you to model complex systems with interacting agents and environments.

Behavior Simulation: Define rules and algorithms to guide agent actions, enabling realistic and adaptable simulations.

Real-World Applications: From urban planning to disaster response, multi-agent simulations provide actionable insights for research and planning.

By mastering multi-agent simulations with LangGraph, you can tackle some of the most challenging questions in research and planning, ensuring your solutions are robust, data-driven, and effective in real-world contexts.

9.3 Industry-Specific Applications

LangGraph's versatility and graph-based structure make it a powerful tool for solving problems across industries. Whether you're optimizing healthcare processes, streamlining logistics, or analyzing financial networks, LangGraph provides a framework to model, simulate, and optimize complex systems. In this section, we'll explore how LangGraph can be applied to three specific industries: healthcare, logistics, and finance. We'll focus on real-world scenarios, practical examples, and the underlying principles that make these applications effective.

Healthcare: Streamlining Patient Flow and Resource Allocation

Healthcare systems are often constrained by limited resources and high demand. Hospitals must manage patient flow, allocate resources efficiently, and ensure timely treatment. LangGraph offers a way to model these processes, identify bottlenecks, and optimize workflows.

Scenario: Managing Patient Flow in an Emergency Department

In a busy emergency department (ED), patients are triaged, treated, and either admitted or discharged. Let's model this process in LangGraph.

Step 1: Modeling the Workflow

We begin by representing key areas of the ED as nodes and the movement of patients as edges.

```
import langgraph

# Create a graph for the ED workflow
hospital = langgraph.Graph()

# Add departments
hospital.add_node("Triage", capacity=10,
type="department")
hospital.add_node("Treatment", capacity=5,
type="department")
hospital.add_node("Admission", capacity=15,
type="department")
```

```
hospital.add_node("Discharge", capacity=20,
type="department")

# Add transitions
hospital.add_edge("Triage", "Treatment",
transition_time=5)
hospital.add_edge("Treatment", "Admission",
transition_time=10)
hospital.add_edge("Treatment", "Discharge",
transition_time=7)

# Display the workflow
print("Emergency Department Workflow:")
for node, data in hospital.nodes(data=True):
    print(f"{node}: {data}")
```

Here:

Each department has a capacity, representing the maximum number of patients it can handle.

Transitions between departments have a transition_time, reflecting the average time to move patients.

Step 2: Simulating Patient Flow

Next, we simulate patient movement through the ED, ensuring that capacities are respected.

```
# Simulate patient flow
def move_patient(graph, current, next_department):
    """Move a patient between departments."""
    if graph.nodes[next_department]["capacity"] >
0:
        graph.nodes[next_department]["capacity"] -=
1
        print(f"Patient moved from {current} to
{next_department}. Remaining capacity in
{next_department}:
{graph.nodes[next_department]['capacity']}")
    else:
        print(f"{next_department} is at full
capacity. Patient cannot move.")
```

```
# Example: Move a patient from Triage to Treatment
move_patient(hospital, "Triage", "Treatment")
```

This simulation provides insights into potential bottlenecks, helping administrators adjust capacities or reallocate resources.

Logistics: Optimizing Supply Chains and Delivery Networks

In logistics, efficiency is paramount. Companies must minimize delivery times, reduce costs, and maximize resource utilization. LangGraph helps model supply chains and delivery networks to identify optimal routes and improve overall performance.

Scenario: Delivery Optimization for an E-Commerce Business

An e-commerce company delivers products from warehouses to customers. Let's create a delivery network and optimize delivery routes.

Step 1: Building the Delivery Network

```
# Create a delivery network
delivery_network = langgraph.Graph()

# Add warehouses and customers
delivery_network.add_node("Warehouse A",
inventory=100)
delivery_network.add_node("Customer 1", demand=10)
delivery_network.add_node("Customer 2", demand=20)

# Add delivery routes with distances
delivery_network.add_edge("Warehouse A", "Customer
1", distance=5)
delivery_network.add_edge("Warehouse A", "Customer
2", distance=8)

# Display the network
print("\nDelivery Network:")
for node, data in
delivery_network.nodes(data=True):
    print(f"{node}: {data}")
```

Step 2: Optimizing Routes

To optimize deliveries, we calculate the shortest path from the warehouse to each customer based on distance.

```python
import networkx as nx

# Convert LangGraph to NetworkX for pathfinding
nx_delivery =
nx.convert_node_labels_to_integers(delivery_network
)

# Find the shortest path for deliveries
def find_shortest_path(graph, source, target):
    """Find the shortest path between source and
target."""
    path = nx.shortest_path(graph, source=source,
target=target, weight="distance")
    print(f"Shortest path from {source} to
{target}: {path}")

# Example: Find the shortest path for deliveries
find_shortest_path(nx_delivery, 0, 1)  # Warehouse
A to Customer 1
find_shortest_path(nx_delivery, 0, 2)  # Warehouse
A to Customer 2
```

By identifying the shortest paths, the company can reduce delivery times and fuel costs.

Finance: Analyzing Fraud and Network Risks

In finance, networks of transactions, accounts, and institutions can be represented as graphs. LangGraph enables fraud detection, risk analysis, and system optimization through graph modeling.

Scenario: Detecting Fraud in Financial Transactions

Fraud detection involves analyzing transaction networks to identify suspicious patterns. Let's model a network of accounts and transactions.

Step 1: Creating the Transaction Network

```python
# Create a transaction network
```

```
transaction_network = langgraph.Graph()

# Add accounts
transaction_network.add_node("Account A",
balance=1000)
transaction_network.add_node("Account B",
balance=2000)

# Add transactions
transaction_network.add_edge("Account A", "Account
B", amount=500, flagged=False)

# Display the network
print("\nTransaction Network:")
for edge in transaction_network.edges(data=True):
    print(edge)
```

Step 2: Detecting Suspicious Transactions

Transactions exceeding a certain threshold may be flagged as suspicious.

```
# Detect suspicious transactions
def detect_fraud(graph, threshold=400):
    """Flag transactions exceeding the
threshold."""
    for u, v, data in graph.edges(data=True):
        if data["amount"] > threshold:
            data["flagged"] = True
            print(f"Suspicious transaction
detected: {u} -> {v}, Amount: {data['amount']}")

# Run fraud detection
detect_fraud(transaction_network)
```

This approach provides a clear, actionable method for identifying and mitigating risks in financial systems.

Healthcare: LangGraph optimizes patient flow, reduces bottlenecks, and ensures efficient resource allocation.

Logistics: Delivery networks benefit from optimized routes and reduced operational costs.

Finance: Fraud detection and risk analysis are simplified through transaction network modeling.

By applying LangGraph to these industry-specific scenarios, you can address real-world challenges with precision, making your systems smarter, faster, and more efficient.

Chapter 10: Performance Optimization and Debugging

Creating intelligent systems using LangGraph requires more than just building workflows and simulations; ensuring they perform efficiently and remain free of issues is equally important. In this chapter, we'll explore techniques for optimizing graph performance, debugging multi-agent systems, and deploying large-scale solutions effectively. Each section is designed to equip you with practical strategies, complete with examples and real-world insights.

10.1 Optimizing Graph Performance

When working with LangGraph, performance optimization becomes increasingly important as graphs grow in size and complexity. Whether you're dealing with thousands of nodes and edges or executing resource-intensive algorithms, optimizing performance ensures your system remains efficient and scalable. In this section, we'll explore practical strategies for improving graph performance, supported by clear explanations, authentic code examples, and relatable real-world scenarios.

Performance bottlenecks in graphs typically arise from three main challenges:

Large Graph Size: As graphs grow, memory usage and processing time increase significantly.

Complex Queries: Tasks like finding shortest paths, calculating centrality, or analyzing connectivity can become computationally expensive.

Inefficient Data Structures: Poorly structured graphs or redundant data can slow down operations.

Optimization addresses these challenges by streamlining the graph structure, leveraging efficient algorithms, and using appropriate data representations.

1. Simplify Graph Structure

A simplified graph structure not only reduces memory usage but also speeds up computations. One effective technique is using edge attributes to store additional information instead of creating extra nodes.

Example: Simplifying Graph Representation

Let's model a transportation network with travel times between locations. Instead of adding nodes for each piece of metadata, we use edge attributes.

```
import langgraph

# Create a transportation graph
transport_graph = langgraph.Graph()

# Add locations as nodes
transport_graph.add_node("City A")
transport_graph.add_node("City B")
transport_graph.add_node("City C")

# Add edges with travel times as attributes
transport_graph.add_edge("City A", "City B",
travel_time=5)
transport_graph.add_edge("City B", "City C",
travel_time=8)
transport_graph.add_edge("City A", "City C",
travel_time=10)

# Display the graph structure
print("Transportation Network:")
for edge in transport_graph.edges(data=True):
    print(edge)
```

Here, instead of creating a separate node for travel time, it's stored as an attribute on the edge, reducing the graph's complexity while preserving all necessary data.

2. Use Sparse Representations for Large Graphs

When dealing with large graphs with many nodes but few connections (sparse graphs), storing the entire adjacency matrix can be wasteful. Sparse matrices, which store only non-zero elements, provide a more efficient representation.

Example: Creating a Sparse Matrix

```
from scipy.sparse import csr_matrix

# Define an adjacency matrix
adj_matrix = csr_matrix([
    [0, 5, 10],
    [0, 0, 8],
    [0, 0, 0]
])

# Display the sparse matrix
print("\nSparse Adjacency Matrix:")
print(adj_matrix)
```

Sparse matrices significantly reduce memory usage and speed up computations for large-scale systems like social networks or transportation grids.

3. Precompute Expensive Calculations

For metrics or queries that don't change frequently, precomputing and caching the results can save significant computation time.

Example: Precomputing Shortest Paths

Let's precompute the shortest paths for all pairs of nodes in a weighted graph.

```
import networkx as nx

# Create a NetworkX graph for shortest path
analysis
nx_graph = nx.Graph()
nx_graph.add_weighted_edges_from([
    ("City A", "City B", 5),
    ("City B", "City C", 8),
    ("City A", "City C", 10)
])

# Precompute all shortest paths
shortest_paths =
dict(nx.all_pairs_dijkstra_path_length(nx_graph))
```

```
# Store precomputed paths
print("\nPrecomputed Shortest Paths:")
for node, paths in shortest_paths.items():
    print(f"{node}: {paths}")
```

Storing precomputed paths allows you to retrieve results instantly instead of recalculating them repeatedly.

4. Optimize Algorithms and Queries

Choosing the right algorithm can make a significant difference in performance. For example, breadth-first search (BFS) is ideal for unweighted graphs, while Dijkstra's algorithm is more efficient for weighted graphs.

Example: Efficient Pathfinding

```
# Find the shortest path using Dijkstra's algorithm
source, target = "City A", "City C"
path_length = nx.dijkstra_path_length(nx_graph,
source=source, target=target, weight="weight")

print(f"\nShortest path from {source} to {target}:
{path_length}")
```

Selecting the optimal algorithm for your graph's characteristics reduces computation time and improves scalability.

Real-World Example: Social Network Analysis

In social networks, nodes represent users, and edges represent relationships or interactions. Optimizing performance is essential for tasks like identifying influencers or detecting communities.

Scenario: Identifying Influencers

We'll calculate the degree centrality of each user to identify those with the most connections.

```
# Create a social network graph
social_network = langgraph.Graph()
```

```python
# Add users and relationships
social_network.add_edges_from([
    ("User A", "User B"),
    ("User A", "User C"),
    ("User B", "User D"),
    ("User C", "User D"),
    ("User D", "User E")
])

# Calculate degree centrality
degree_centrality =
nx.degree_centrality(social_network)
print("\nDegree Centrality:")
for user, centrality in degree_centrality.items():
    print(f"{user}: {centrality:.2f}")
```

Precomputing and caching these metrics ensures efficient querying in large-scale networks.

5. Parallelize Graph Operations

For extremely large graphs, parallel processing can distribute workloads across multiple CPUs or machines, reducing runtime significantly.

Example: Parallel Pathfinding with Dask

```python
from dask import delayed, compute

# Define parallel tasks for pathfinding
@delayed
def parallel_path(source, target):
    return nx.dijkstra_path_length(nx_graph,
source=source, target=target, weight="weight")

# Execute pathfinding in parallel
tasks = [parallel_path("City A", "City B"),
parallel_path("City B", "City C")]
results = compute(*tasks)

print("\nParallel Pathfinding Results:", results)
```

By leveraging parallelism, you can handle computationally intensive tasks efficiently, even for massive graphs.

Simplify Structures: Use edge attributes and sparse representations to streamline your graph.

Precompute and Cache: Store frequently used metrics and results to save computational time.

Leverage Efficient Algorithms: Choose algorithms that match your graph's characteristics, such as BFS for unweighted graphs or Dijkstra's for weighted graphs.

Utilize Parallel Processing: Distribute workloads across multiple CPUs or machines for large-scale graphs.

By applying these techniques, you can optimize LangGraph for performance, ensuring your systems are both efficient and scalable, no matter the size or complexity of your graphs.

10.2 Troubleshooting Multi-Agent Systems

Multi-agent systems are powerful but complex, as they involve multiple autonomous agents working together, often in dynamic and unpredictable environments. When something goes wrong in such systems, identifying and resolving the issue can be challenging. Effective troubleshooting requires a systematic approach to diagnosing problems, analyzing agent behaviors, and validating system integrity.

Before jumping into troubleshooting, let's understand the types of problems that can arise in multi-agent systems:

State Inconsistencies: Agents might enter invalid states or fail to transition correctly due to logic errors.

Communication Failures: Agents may lose connectivity or fail to share critical information.

Task Deadlocks: Dependencies between tasks can cause agents to wait indefinitely for one another.

Unintended Behaviors: Agents might act in ways that conflict with their goals due to misconfigured rules or priorities.

Now that we've outlined the potential pitfalls, let's address how to identify and fix them.

1. Monitoring Agent States

Tracking the state of each agent is essential for identifying inconsistencies. By logging transitions and current states, you can quickly spot when an agent behaves unexpectedly.

Example: Logging Agent States

Let's create a simple system where agents move between states such as idle, working, and completed.

```python
# Define agents and their states
agents = {
    "Agent 1": {"state": "idle", "task": None},
    "Agent 2": {"state": "working", "task": "Task A"},
}

# Function to update and log agent states
def update_agent_state(agent, new_state,
task=None):
    old_state = agents[agent]["state"]
    agents[agent]["state"] = new_state
    agents[agent]["task"] = task
    print(f"{agent}: State changed from {old_state}
to {new_state}. Task: {task}")

# Example state updates
update_agent_state("Agent 1", "working", "Task B")
update_agent_state("Agent 2", "completed")
```

By logging these transitions, you can identify when an agent enters an invalid or unexpected state.

2. Debugging Communication Failures

Communication is the backbone of multi-agent systems. When agents fail to communicate effectively, tasks may be delayed, duplicated, or dropped entirely.

Example: Testing Agent Communication

Suppose agents use a simple messaging protocol to exchange updates. We can simulate communication and detect failures.

```
# Simulate agent communication
def send_message(sender, receiver, message):
    try:
        # Simulate a communication success or
failure
        response = {"status": "success"}  # Replace
with actual messaging logic
        if response["status"] == "success":
            print(f"{sender} to {receiver}:
{message}")
        else:
            raise ConnectionError
    except ConnectionError:
        print(f"Message from {sender} to {receiver}
failed.")

# Test communication
send_message("Agent 1", "Agent 2", "Task A is
completed.")
```

Regular communication checks and retries ensure that agents stay connected and up-to-date.

3. Resolving Task Deadlocks

Deadlocks occur when agents are waiting for resources or actions from one another in a circular dependency. This can halt the entire system.

Example: Detecting and Resolving Deadlocks

We'll model a scenario where two agents are stuck waiting for each other's tasks to complete.

```
# Define task dependencies
tasks = {
    "Task A": {"status": "pending", "dependent_on":
["Task B"]},
    "Task B": {"status": "pending", "dependent_on":
["Task A"]},
}
```

```
# Function to detect deadlocks
def detect_deadlock(task_graph):
    for task, details in task_graph.items():
        for dependency in details["dependent_on"]:
            if
task_graph[dependency]["dependent_on"].count(task)
> 0:
                print(f"Deadlock detected between
{task} and {dependency}.")
                return True
    return False

# Detect deadlocks
if detect_deadlock(tasks):
    print("Resolving deadlock by reassigning
tasks...")
    tasks["Task A"]["dependent_on"] = []
    tasks["Task B"]["dependent_on"] = []
```

Breaking dependencies or reassigning tasks can resolve deadlocks, ensuring progress continues.

4. Validating Agent Behaviors

Agents often operate based on predefined rules or goals. Misconfigurations can cause them to act counterproductively. Validating agent behaviors ensures they align with system objectives.

Example: Behavior Validation

Let's define rules for agent behavior and validate them during execution.

```
# Define agent rules
agent_rules = {
    "Agent 1": {"goal": "complete tasks",
"restricted_actions": ["delete tasks"]},
}

# Validate agent actions
def validate_action(agent, action):
```

```
      if action in
agent_rules[agent]["restricted_actions"]:
         print(f"{agent}: Invalid action '{action}'
detected!")
    else:
         print(f"{agent}: Action '{action}' is
valid.")

# Test validation
validate_action("Agent 1", "complete tasks")
validate_action("Agent 1", "delete tasks")
```

This prevents agents from performing actions that violate system rules or objectives.

Real-World Example: Warehouse Robot Coordination

In a warehouse, robots (agents) work together to pick, pack, and ship items. Let's model and troubleshoot common issues.

Scenario: Robot Task Allocation

```
# Define robot tasks
robots = {
    "Robot 1": {"state": "idle", "task": None},
    "Robot 2": {"state": "working", "task": "Pick
Item A"},
}

tasks = {"Pick Item A": {"status": "pending"},
"Pack Item A": {"status": "pending"}}

# Assign tasks dynamically
def assign_task(robot, task):
    if tasks[task]["status"] == "pending":
        robots[robot]["state"] = "working"
        robots[robot]["task"] = task
        tasks[task]["status"] = "assigned"
        print(f"{robot} assigned to {task}.")
    else:
        print(f"{robot}: Task {task} is already
assigned.")
```

```
# Test task assignment
assign_task("Robot 1", "Pick Item A")
assign_task("Robot 2", "Pack Item A")
```

Monitor States: Logging agent states and transitions helps identify inconsistencies and troubleshoot behaviors.

Ensure Communication: Regularly test and validate communication channels to prevent disruptions.

Resolve Deadlocks: Detect circular dependencies and resolve them to maintain progress.

Validate Actions: Ensure agents operate within defined rules and objectives to avoid unintended behaviors.

By systematically monitoring, validating, and troubleshooting your multi-agent system, you ensure it operates reliably, efficiently, and in alignment with its intended goals. This approach minimizes downtime and enhances the system's overall effectiveness.

10.3 Best Practices for Large-Scale Deployments

When scaling LangGraph systems to handle large graphs or multi-agent setups, it's crucial to adopt strategies that ensure reliability, scalability, and maintainability. Large-scale deployments bring unique challenges, such as managing high computational demands, ensuring smooth collaboration between distributed components, and minimizing downtime during updates. In this section, I'll guide you through best practices for deploying LangGraph systems in large-scale environments.

Design for Scalability

Scalability ensures your system can handle increased workloads without degrading performance. It requires careful planning from the outset to ensure your architecture can grow as needed.

Horizontal Scaling with Distributed Systems

In large-scale deployments, distributing workloads across multiple machines or nodes helps balance processing demands. Tools like **Dask** or **Apache Spark** can partition and process graph workloads in parallel.

Example: Parallel Graph Processing with Dask

Let's distribute a large graph across multiple workers for parallel computation.

```
from dask.distributed import Client
import networkx as nx
import dask.bag as db

# Start a Dask client
client = Client()

# Create a large graph
large_graph = nx.erdos_renyi_graph(1000, 0.01)   #
1000 nodes, 1% edge probability

# Partition graph into smaller subgraphs
subgraphs =
list(nx.connected_components(large_graph))
subgraph_bag = db.from_sequence(subgraphs)

# Process subgraphs in parallel
def compute_subgraph_metrics(subgraph):
    return len(subgraph),
nx.diameter(nx.subgraph(large_graph, subgraph))

results =
subgraph_bag.map(compute_subgraph_metrics).compute(
)
print("Metrics for subgraphs:", results)
```

Here:

Connected components are treated as independent subgraphs.

Each subgraph is processed in parallel, reducing computation time for large graphs.

Optimize Resource Utilization

Efficient resource management is essential for large-scale systems to minimize costs and ensure smooth operation.

Load Balancing

Distribute workloads evenly across nodes to avoid overloading any single machine. For example, in a multi-agent system, you can use task queues to allocate tasks dynamically based on resource availability.

Example: Dynamic Task Allocation

```python
# Define agents and task queue
agents = {"Agent 1": {"capacity": 5}, "Agent 2":
{"capacity": 3}}
tasks = [{"name": "Task A", "size": 2}, {"name":
"Task B", "size": 3}, {"name": "Task C", "size":
4}]

# Allocate tasks dynamically
def allocate_tasks(agents, tasks):
    for task in tasks:
        for agent, data in agents.items():
            if data["capacity"] >= task["size"]:
                data["capacity"] -= task["size"]
                print(f"{agent} assigned
{task['name']}. Remaining capacity:
{data['capacity']}")
                break
        else:
            print(f"Task {task['name']} could not
be assigned.")

allocate_tasks(agents, tasks)
```

This ensures that tasks are allocated efficiently without exceeding agent capacity.

Ensure High Availability

High availability minimizes downtime, ensuring that your system remains operational even during failures or maintenance.

Implement Failover Mechanisms

Failover systems automatically redirect tasks to backup nodes if a primary node fails. This keeps the system functional during unexpected disruptions.

Example: Task Failover

```
# Simulate failover
primary_node = {"status": "down"}
backup_node = {"status": "active", "capacity": 10}

def handle_failover(primary, backup, task):
    if primary["status"] != "active":
        print(f"Primary node unavailable.
Redirecting {task} to backup node.")
        backup["capacity"] -= 1
    else:
        print(f"Task {task} handled by primary
node.")

handle_failover(primary_node, backup_node,
"Critical Task")
```

By seamlessly transferring workloads, failover systems enhance reliability.

Streamline Updates and Maintenance

Large-scale deployments often require regular updates. Minimize downtime by implementing techniques like rolling updates or blue-green deployments.

Rolling Updates

In a rolling update, parts of the system are updated incrementally while others remain operational. This avoids service disruption.

Example: Rolling Update Simulation

```
# Define nodes in the system
nodes = [{"id": 1, "version": "v1"}, {"id": 2,
"version": "v1"}, {"id": 3, "version": "v1"}]

# Perform a rolling update
def rolling_update(nodes, new_version):
```

```
    for node in nodes:
        print(f"Updating Node {node['id']} to
{new_version}...")
        node["version"] = new_version
        print(f"Node {node['id']} updated
successfully.")

rolling_update(nodes, "v2")
```

This ensures that only a subset of nodes is affected at any given time.

Monitor and Analyze System Performance

Continuous monitoring allows you to detect and address issues proactively. Use tools like **Prometheus** or **Grafana** for metrics collection and visualization.

Log Agent Activities

Tracking agent activities helps identify bottlenecks and inefficiencies.

Example: Logging Agent Metrics

```
# Simulate agent activity logging
agent_logs = []

def log_activity(agent, action):
    agent_logs.append({"agent": agent, "action":
action})
    print(f"{agent}: {action}")

log_activity("Agent 1", "Completed Task A")
log_activity("Agent 2", "Started Task B")

print("\nAgent Logs:", agent_logs)
```

These logs can be aggregated and analyzed for performance insights.

Real-World Example: Logistics Network Deployment

Let's consider a logistics network with warehouses and delivery agents. To scale the system:

Distribute Deliveries: Assign deliveries to agents dynamically based on their current load and location.

Optimize Routes: Use shortest-path algorithms for efficient navigation.

Monitor Performance: Track agent delivery times and success rates.

Implementation

```python
# Define warehouses and agents
warehouses = {"Warehouse 1": {"location": (0, 0),
"capacity": 100}}
agents = {"Agent 1": {"location": (1, 1),
"capacity": 5}, "Agent 2": {"location": (2, 2),
"capacity": 3}}

# Optimize delivery assignments
def assign_delivery(warehouses, agents,
deliveries):
    for delivery in deliveries:
        closest_agent = min(
            agents,
            key=lambda agent:
((agents[agent]["location"][0] -
warehouses[delivery["warehouse"]]["location"][0])
** 2
                                +
(agents[agent]["location"][1] -
warehouses[delivery["warehouse"]]["location"][1])
** 2)
        )
        print(f"Assigned {delivery['id']} to
{closest_agent}.")

# Example deliveries
deliveries = [{"id": "Delivery 1", "warehouse":
"Warehouse 1"}]
assign_delivery(warehouses, agents, deliveries)
```

This combines scalability, optimization, and monitoring for efficient logistics management.

Design for Scalability: Use distributed systems and parallel processing to handle large-scale graphs and workloads.

Optimize Resources: Balance workloads dynamically to maximize efficiency.

Ensure Availability: Implement failover mechanisms and rolling updates to maintain system reliability.

Monitor Continuously: Collect and analyze metrics to detect and resolve performance issues proactively.

By following these best practices, you can deploy LangGraph systems at scale, ensuring they are robust, efficient, and ready to meet the demands of real-world applications.

Chapter 11: Trends in Intelligent Agents and Multi-Agent Systems

As artificial intelligence continues to evolve, intelligent agents and multi-agent systems (MAS) are becoming increasingly important. These systems are no longer just research concepts but key components in industries ranging from healthcare to finance and beyond. In this chapter, we'll explore the latest trends shaping intelligent agents and multi-agent systems and the future directions they're likely to take.

By blending emerging technologies with practical insights, this discussion will help you understand how to leverage these advancements for building more robust, adaptive, and scalable AI workflows.

11.1 Emerging Technologies in AI Workflows

AI workflows have advanced significantly due to innovations in machine learning, natural language processing, distributed computing, and edge intelligence. These technologies are redefining how agents operate, communicate, and solve problems.

1. Integration of Large Language Models (LLMs)

Large Language Models like OpenAI's GPT series and Google's Bard are transforming how agents process and generate human language. These models enable agents to:

Understand context better.

Handle nuanced interactions.

Generate coherent and relevant responses.

Example: Using LLMs in a Multi-Agent System

Imagine a customer service system where agents handle user queries in natural language. One agent handles text parsing, while another retrieves data from a knowledge base.

```
from transformers import pipeline

# Load a language model for text parsing
nlp = pipeline("question-answering")
```

```
# Define a question and context
context = "The LangGraph system can model workflows
and multi-agent interactions efficiently."
question = "What can LangGraph model?"

# Process the query
result = nlp(question=question, context=context)
print(f"Answer: {result['answer']}")
```

This capability empowers agents to interact seamlessly with users, providing accurate and contextually relevant information.

2. Distributed Intelligence

Distributed intelligence ensures that agents operate efficiently across a network, leveraging decentralized decision-making and resource sharing. With frameworks like **Ray** and **Apache Kafka**, agents can process tasks concurrently, reducing latency and improving scalability.

Real-World Scenario: Traffic Management

In a smart city, distributed agents manage traffic lights at intersections. Each agent communicates with neighboring intersections to optimize traffic flow dynamically.

```
# Simulate a distributed traffic management system
import random

agents = {"Intersection 1": {"state": "green"},
"Intersection 2": {"state": "red"}}

def update_traffic(agent, neighbors):
    # Simulate traffic updates based on neighbor
states
    if neighbors["Intersection 2"]["state"] ==
"green":
        agents[agent]["state"] = "red"
    else:
        agents[agent]["state"] = "green"
    print(f"{agent}: State updated to
{agents[agent]['state']}.")
```

```
# Update traffic states
update_traffic("Intersection 1", agents)
update_traffic("Intersection 2", agents)
```

This decentralized approach minimizes bottlenecks and improves overall system efficiency.

3. Edge AI and IoT Integration

Edge AI allows agents to process data locally on edge devices, reducing reliance on centralized servers. This is especially useful for latency-sensitive applications like autonomous vehicles or industrial robots.

Real-World Application: Predictive Maintenance

Industrial robots equipped with edge AI can monitor their own performance and predict maintenance needs. For instance, an agent detects anomalies in motor vibrations using local sensors.

```
# Simulate predictive maintenance using local
sensors
import numpy as np

# Simulated vibration data
vibration_data = np.random.normal(loc=0, scale=1,
size=100)

# Detect anomalies
anomalies = [v for v in vibration_data if abs(v) >
2]
if anomalies:
    print(f"Anomalies detected: {len(anomalies)}")
else:
    print("System operating normally.")
```

By processing data locally, agents can act quickly to prevent failures.

11.2 Future Prospects of Multi-Agent Systems

The future of multi-agent systems is shaped by advances in technology and their integration into increasingly complex environments. Key areas of growth include enhanced collaboration, autonomous learning, and ethical AI.

1. Autonomous Collaboration

Future agents will collaborate autonomously, sharing resources and knowledge to achieve common goals. For instance, in disaster response scenarios, drone swarms could map affected areas and deliver supplies collaboratively.

Scenario: Drone Swarm for Disaster Relief

```
# Define drones and tasks
drones = {"Drone 1": {"location": (0, 0)}, "Drone
2": {"location": (10, 10)}}
tasks = [{"location": (5, 5), "priority": "high"},
{"location": (15, 15), "priority": "low"}]

# Assign tasks to drones
def assign_task(drones, tasks):
    for task in tasks:
        closest_drone = min(drones, key=lambda d:
(drones[d]["location"][0] - task["location"][0]) **
2 +
                                                    (
drones[d]["location"][1] - task["location"][1]) **
2)
        print(f"{closest_drone} assigned to task at
{task['location']}.")

assign_task(drones, tasks)
```

Autonomous collaboration reduces response times and ensures resources are utilized effectively.

2. Lifelong Learning Agents

Future agents will learn continuously from their environments, improving their capabilities over time without requiring explicit reprogramming. This is achieved through reinforcement learning and neural networks.

Example: Reinforcement Learning for Task Optimization

```
import random

# Define states and rewards
states = ["idle", "working", "completed"]
rewards = {"working": 1, "completed": 10}

# Simulate learning process
def simulate_learning(agent_state):
    if agent_state == "working":
        reward = rewards["working"]
    elif agent_state == "completed":
        reward = rewards["completed"]
    else:
        reward = 0
    print(f"Agent in state '{agent_state}' received
reward: {reward}")

simulate_learning("working")
simulate_learning("completed")
```

Lifelong learning enables agents to adapt to new challenges dynamically.

3. Ethical AI in Multi-Agent Systems

As agents become more autonomous, ensuring ethical decision-making is critical. Systems must be designed to prioritize fairness, transparency, and accountability.

Example: Ethical Decision-Making in Healthcare

In healthcare, agents assist in triaging patients. Ethical rules ensure that decisions are based on urgency, not external biases.

```
# Simulate ethical triage
patients = [{"id": 1, "urgency": 5}, {"id": 2,
"urgency": 9}, {"id": 3, "urgency": 3}]

# Sort patients by urgency
patients.sort(key=lambda p: p["urgency"],
reverse=True)
print("Patients triaged by urgency:", patients)
```

By embedding ethical principles, agents maintain trust and accountability.

Emerging Technologies: LLMs, distributed intelligence, and edge AI are revolutionizing AI workflows and agent capabilities.

Future Trends: Multi-agent systems will focus on autonomous collaboration, lifelong learning, and ethical decision-making.

Real-World Applications: From disaster response to predictive maintenance and healthcare, intelligent agents are becoming indispensable.

By staying informed about these trends and technologies, you'll be equipped to design systems that are not only cutting-edge but also scalable, ethical, and impactful in real-world settings.

Conclusion

The journey through this book has been an exploration of the fascinating and rapidly evolving world of intelligent agents, multi-agent systems, and graph-based AI workflows. From foundational concepts to advanced techniques, we have delved into the mechanics, applications, and potential of LangGraph as a framework for creating dynamic, efficient, and intelligent systems.

At its core, this book aimed to provide you with not only theoretical insights but also practical tools to implement real-world solutions. By understanding the anatomy of intelligent agents, modeling workflows, integrating machine learning, and optimizing distributed systems, you are now equipped to tackle complex challenges in domains as diverse as healthcare, logistics, finance, and beyond.

Intelligent agents are no longer confined to theoretical constructs or niche applications. They are driving innovation across industries, enabling systems to make decisions, adapt to dynamic environments, and collaborate with one another. The potential of multi-agent systems to simulate and manage complex, interdependent tasks is reshaping how we approach problem-solving in AI.

LangGraph, as a graph-based framework, stands at the intersection of these advancements, offering a flexible and scalable solution for modeling workflows and interactions. Its ability to integrate with emerging technologies, such as machine learning and edge computing, ensures that it remains relevant in a rapidly changing technological landscape.

The future of intelligent systems and LangGraph is rich with possibilities:

Emerging Technologies: The integration of large language models, distributed intelligence, and edge AI will further enhance the capabilities of agents and workflows.

Scalability: Innovations in distributed systems and real-time collaboration will make LangGraph suitable for even larger and more complex deployments.

Ethics and Sustainability: As AI systems become more autonomous, embedding ethical principles and ensuring transparency will be crucial for maintaining trust and fairness.

While these advancements promise exciting opportunities, they also demand thoughtful implementation and continuous learning. As a practitioner, researcher, or enthusiast, your role in shaping the future of LangGraph and intelligent systems is vital.

This book is not just a guide—it's an invitation. You are now part of a growing community of innovators who are pushing the boundaries of what intelligent systems can achieve. Whether you're building cutting-edge AI workflows, contributing to the development of LangGraph, or applying these concepts to solve real-world problems, your efforts contribute to a larger mission: making technology smarter, more adaptable, and more human-centric.

Remember, the possibilities of LangGraph and intelligent agents are limited only by imagination and innovation. As you move forward, continue to experiment, collaborate, and share your knowledge. Together, we can build systems that not only solve today's challenges but also anticipate the needs of tomorrow.

The journey does not end here. It begins with your ideas, your projects, and your contributions. LangGraph is a tool, a framework, and a philosophy—a way to think about systems as interconnected, adaptive, and intelligent.

As you close this book, I encourage you to take what you've learned and create something extraordinary. The world of intelligent agents and multi-agent systems is vast, and your role in it is critical. Embrace the opportunity to innovate, collaborate, and lead. The future is waiting, and with LangGraph, you have the tools to shape it.

Thank you for joining me on this journey. Let's build the future—together.